VENETIAN VILLAS

Original title: Città delle ville venete

All rights of reproduction, in the whole or in part, of the text
or the illustrations are reserved throughout the world.

© 1999 for this 2nd revised English language edition
Könemann Verlagsgesellschaft mbH
Bonner Strasse 126, D - 50968 Cologne

Translation into English: Peter Lauritzen, John Harper, Stephen Sartarelli
Typesetting: Goodfellow & Egan, Cambridge
Production Manager: Detlev Schaper
Production: Mark Voges
Printing and Binding: Neue Stalling, Oldenburg

Printed in Germany
ISBN 3-89508-242-2

10 9 8 7 6 5 4 3 2 1

MICHELANGELO MURANO, PAOLO MARTON

VENETIAN VILLAS

KÖNEMANN

CONTENTS

Introduction

The richness and depth of the research conducted by Michelangelo Muraro on *Venetian Villas* is the fruit of a career devoted entirely to the study of all aspects of Venetian art, to university instruction, and to the conservation of monuments, paints, and sculpture, in the roles of director of the Department of Monuments of Venice and Venetia and museum director of the Museo della Ca' d'Oro in Venice.

His kind invitation to write these words of introduction gives me an opportunity to extend thanks to him on behalf of scholarly colleagues of all nationalities, for having so generously shared with us his knowledge of Venetian art and culture, and the pleasure of his conversation.

In the present volume, embellished with the spectacular photographs of Paolo Marton, Mr Muraro gives an indication of the studious efforts through which he has, over the last twenty years, helped us come to know what he calls the "Culture of the Venetian Villas."

He was in fact the first to take up this subject, which previously had barely attracted the attention of such scholars as Wittkower, Pane, and Zorsi, who limited their studies exclusively to the work of Palladio. Not until the early 1950s was a broader interest awakened, when, with a number of exhibitions devoted to Venetian Villas, Michelangelo Muraro, along with Renato Ceves and Guiseppe Mazzotti, emerged as the central figure of this revival. And it was precisely to Michelangelo Muraro that fell the task of exporting these exhibitions to France and America.

The idea of the "Culture of the Venetian Villas" met with great success; this was due in part to a profound shift of interest in the field of art history. From its initial concentration on questions of stylistic definition – essential in the formative period of our discipline to assigning the attribution and determining the chronology of artworks – which encouraged monographic studies on individual artists, research has subsequently moved towards an interpretation of art in relation to its social, political, economic, and cultural context.

The importance of Muraro's contribution toward this end is demonstrated in the text contained herein, which served as a guide to Paolo Marton in his painstaking photographic campaigns across the entire region.

"Culture" [*Civiltà*], as Muraro suggests, is a broad concept; one which embraces all aspects of human endeavor, especially the manner in which man weaves his relations with the natural environment. The art historian is, in this respect, in a position to interpret the various different aspects of the "human sciences." The value of these texts lies above all in their ability to interpret, in a unified manner, the most disparate historical forces as they interact in the formation of a culture: the social structure, the relations to the domestic and foreign political situation, the economic realities, the technologies, the road systems, the topography and use of the terrain, philosophy, literature, and painting.

At the basis of Muraro's interpretation of the Venetian villas is his indigenous familiarity with the territory. He was in fact born and raised in a country town in the Vicenza province. His experience of villas, therefore, appears to be deeply rooted in these places, whose characteristics he knows very well – roads, rivers, canals, and above all, the way in which the working of the water system and the gradual draining of the marshes contributed to the development of the agricultural economy as a foundation for the rise of the villas.

The term "reclamation" appears repeatedly in these pages; the conquest, through reclamation, of vast stretches of terrain originally unsuitable for cultivation, becomes a key to understanding the extraordinary promptness with which the Venetian nobility of the Renaissance turned their attentions away from maritime commerce and toward the utilization of farming estates on the mainland. This initiative constitutes the main difference between the villas of the Serene Republic and those of Florence or Rome, which were rarely conceived with the purpose of contributing to the economy and only partly served an agricultural purpose.

Muraro shows how this shift in objectives was not solely motivated by the desires of private citizens to obtain personal gain, but was above all dictated by the need for the Republic to ensure its self-sufficiency in times of war and to protect itself from famine.

This phenomenon also has its intellectual side, which was clearly formulated in the writings of Alvise Cornaro, a Paduan humanist of the early Cinquecento. This passionate promoter of land reclamation tried to raise agriculture to the level of an art which, because of its ethical ends, would appear worthy of being practicsed by the nobility itself, according to the guiding principles set forth by a writer of republican Rome, Cato.

Venice, in the meanwhile, saw its own awareness of being heir to ancient Rome grow during the formative period of the villa culture. Venetian villas drew inspiration from those built in the Roman provinces, even though medieval and Renaissance builders could not have had any direct knowledge of the ancient models.

Palladio's villas illustrate the complexity of this "culture," which combined the results of scientific research into Roman texts and monuments with elements of traditional Venetian farms and forms derived from medieval castles.

One important contribution of Muraro's is his recognition of the import of the persistence of the feudal system in the Venetian countryside and in the orbit of the villas. It has in fact been shown that, starting in the late Middle Ages, feudal rights on the mainland were not only passed on from father to son (through customary succession), but could also be passed on to the eventual buyer of the fief. As a result, Venetian merchants could buy landed property and obtain a noble title in the bargain; the Doge, in accordance with a fourteenth-century agreement, would confirm them as vassals of the Holy Roman Empire.

This opportunity must have increased the demand for landed property on the part of members of the Venetian ruling class, who up to that point, as citizens of the Republic, had been unable to acquire noble titles through services rendered to the state. They were no doubt annoyed by the fact that representatives of the most influential families of Vicenza, Verona, and other mainland cities (that had been pro-Empire until Venetian preeminence in the fifteenth century) possessed fiefs and ancient titles of Imperial nobility.

The question of the self-assertion of the classes comes up often in these pages. Indeed, since ancient Roman times, the ideology of the villa has taken the shape of a myth of the benefits and pleasures of country life, a myth cultivated by the urban bourgeoisie that the farmer, serf, or small landowner could not allow himself to indulge in, as Goldoni repeatedly points out.

The reader, confronted with the variety of scholarly disciplines that form the basis of the arguments contained in this book, might get the mistaken impression that they are nothing more than a series of subtle academic exercises. Though they are indeed subtle, they are far from academic in nature.

The text of *Venetian Villas* is structured almost like an impressionistic tapestry, around the weft of which many different threads are freely woven; one observation might be drawn from an archival document, another from the author's own imagination or sensibility.

The style is therefore quite different from that found in academic journals. In certain "illuminating" passages it is comparable to the sort of approach that Lévi-Strauss, in *La pensée sauvage*, called *bricolage* – that is, a manner of constructing an argument based on traditional elements and at the same time on myth and sensorial reactions, and constituting a stimulating alternative to scientific analysis.

Comparisons aside, these studies offer a wide range of rich and varied experiences that produce in the reader a deep understanding of the significance of this "Culture" [*Civiltà*] that goes beyond the keen desire to visit, perhaps on foot, all of the places mentioned or illustrated in this book.

James S. Ackerman
Professor of Fine Arts
Harvard University
Cambridge, MA.

The Venetia of the Villas

The title chosen for this volume, "Venetian Villas" indicates a desire to explore the phenomenon of the villa in all the variety and richness of its components, as a symbol of the mentality and history of an entire region.

It is not perhaps irrelevant to the conception of this work that I live and work in Venice, while having spent my childhood in the Venetian countryside.

Alongside the ancient testimonies, the words of the writers cited almost as keys to understanding the individual chapters, the loving pages that G. Comisso and G. Piovene devoted to the landscape and people of Venetia were of equal importance to me. I am indeed convinced that, as G. Duby has maintained, the faculty of the imagination aids one in rediscovering the context of an epoch and in reorganizing into a unified vision all the uncertain and fragmentary vestiges that the past has left behind us.

The context of the "Culture of the Venetian villas" itself, which today represents a very precise stage in Venetian history and art, is also the fruit of an acquired awareness of the gradual emergence of a reality that was initially vague and undefined. Historical knowledge, as many maintain nowadays, first arises from feelings or curiosities of various sorts and only secondly looks to scientific support for enrichment.

This long study of villas had, in fact, as its starting point my bond of affection with my native land, the emotion and aesthetic pleasure I feel for the cities populating it, and lastly, my curiosity and eagerness to understand the reasons behind certain architectural solutions and certain economic choices. In attempting to find answers to these questions by studying the hydrography, politics, economics, and nature of the society and culture of the Venetian mainland, what emerged and took shape was the concept of a villa culture spread all across the region, a key episode in any understanding of the history of Venice and of its most lively and enduring sensibilities.

This volume is first and foremost an invitation to anyone visiting or studying Venetia who might be hypnotized by the myth of Venice, by its artistic and cultural treasures and by the changable fascination of the lagoons. It is not enough to see just Venice, isolated there on the sea, if one wants to understand the many-sided variety of its life and history.

An "amphibian" city, she is enriched by her double connotation, her maritime and land identities; and while the former aspect is easily perceived, the latter remains someone obscure and hidden. One must penetrate into the mainland to unveil the secrets of a centuries-old history, to uncover the imprint of the Serene Republic, its contribution in the unification of a territory whose individual provinces nevertheless retained their distinct physiognomies.

Thus our appreciation and gratitude, amply expressed in these pages, goes out to the forefathers and founders of the villa culture – the Venetian legislators and noble patrons, the regional inhabitants who, in the face of difficulties and sacrifices, welcomed the new mentality and established with the villas' proprietors an active relationship of trust and collaboration.

A scholar of Venetian things cannot, therefore, ignore the complex reality of the mainland that one finds documented in the villas, even though in the present day it is no longer possible to reconstruct that splendid culture in its entirety. Lost forever, for example, is the former relationship between the villas and the environment; we need only imagine how prominent they must have once looked, with their noble, durable architects, in contrast with the precarious straw-roofed, wooden structures of the nearby rural homes.

But the losses could have been much worse; for many years, indifference and ignorance caused many of the villas to fall into a state of disrepair, which at a certain point seemed irremediable. If today it is possible for us to enjoy the beauty of these architectural works, to study their histories, and to understand their functions and purposes, the credit must go to the scholars and enthusiasts who, starting in the 1950s with exhibitions, catalogues, and publications, have reawakened an ever-growing interest in the villas, calling for restorations and promoting new initiatives.

Michelangelo Muraro

The Photographs

Almost three years have passed since I began my voyage among the villas of Venetia. During this long period I took thousands of photographs, travelling the roads of Venetia through all of its provinces. Now that the volume is finally ready to go to the printer, I find myself re-reading the pages of my work diary with a bit of nostalgia.

Amid all the technical notes I take pleasure in rediscovering the vivid impressions of some of the more exhausing days, or the observations I made on the best way to approach and resolve certain photographic situations.

I always asked myself, each time I set out to photograph a new villa, what angle would be the ideal one in the mind of the architect himself. In many cases, there was no answer to this question; no doubt that vantage point had once existed, but the changes brought about in the landscape over the centuries had vastly altered the environmental situation, creating obstacles and impediments to a perfect view of the subject. Moreover, the architectural work, which is conceived and situated exclusively in three-dimensional space, cannot always be represented in the entirety of its design when one chooses a single point of view to portray it.

Since the photographic image is obviously two-dimensional, the representation of spatial effects remains dependant on the skilful control of planes and perspectives; such control may be achieved by making use of the specific features of an optimal technical device such as the monorail camera. I therefore concentrated on a choice of framings and lights that would bring out the best in the architecture and its relation to the landscape.

Some of the most admired Venetian villas, such as "Rotonda," the Maser Villa, or the "Rocca Pisana," are still wonderfully visible in their original environmental context, set like splendid jewels in the green of the surrounding hills, just as they were when first designed and built. I waited through all the seasons to find the ideal light for bringing out the harmony of their architecture.

In the shots of interiors, which are essential in a book of this sort, I often had to create the light in the rooms myself, patiently experimenting by arranging and rearranging my lamps in order to accentuate the spatial rhythms and to bring out the full chromatic range of the frescos and decorations, which would have been inaccessible in natural light. Finally, I tried to interpret some of the masterworks of the greats who frescoed the rooms of the villas of Venetia, masters such as Veronese, Zelotti, Fasolo, and the two Tiepolos, father and son.

In studying the details, which I chose through a careful cutting of the whole image, I was truly moved as I rediscovered the extraordinary vitality of these pictures, whose fascination remains unchanged after so many centuries.

To realize the images in this volume I used a *Sinar F* monorail camera, equipped with *Schneider* and *Rodenstock* lenses, backed up by my trusty *Leica*, which I used for specific situations.

I would like to express my gratitude to all the proprietors of the villas presented in this volume for the courtesty and availability they showed me in allowing me to work freely in spaces often intended for private living. I ask all these people – descendants of ancient Venetian noble families, private citizens, foreigners enamoured of Italian art, finance companies, and public institutions – to accept the images in this volume as a heartfelt homage to their kindness and hospitality. Lastly, I must also express a particular word of thanks to my dear friend Luigina Bortolatto who, with her valuable advice, helped me to overcome successfully a rather difficult moment in the planning of this work.

Paolo Marton

I. History

From the Antique to the Renaissance: The Emergence of the Veneto Villas

THE VENETO LANDSCAPE IN THE ROMAN ERA

Historians, in outlining the development of the Veneto villas, have emphasized the fundamental importance of Andrea Palladio. His art illuminated the sixteenth century and remained a model for succeeding centuries, imitated both within and beyond the boundaries of the Veneto and Italy. The increase in villa construction during the eighteenth century has been at the center of much historical research. The great spread of the Veneto villas and their continuity over time has been explored. We believe, however, that it is necessary to examine both the history of the Veneto villas and their prehistory: that it is useful to look into the immediate as well as the deeper reasons for their success. Only by uncovering the deeper reasons, the links that intertwine around an inexhaustible idea, can we understand why this world of the villas has been reaffirmed and consolidated over the centuries, and thereby understand its peculiarities.

The essential program of the villa (distinct from the simple farm in that considerations of pleasure dominate those of utility) has remained unaltered for over two thousand years, since the time when it was defined by the patricians of ancient Rome. As Ackerman says, they were satisfying a need both

A villa with a fish pond in the background, a Roman mosaic from the Alexandrian period (Venice, Museo Archeologico). Martial comments that the banks of the Alto Adriatico were dotted with luxurious villas.

"psychological and ideological" of the city dweller who conceives of the country not only as an area for possible investment, but also as a place for amusement, relaxation, rest, and study.

But, in an amphibian city like Venice, the need of man to live with nature, to own a piece of land, assumes a particular value and importance. The subtle nostalgia for the terra firma, which characterizes the lagoon city through the centuries, is not without profound repercussions. Nor is it insignificant that Venice, while never forgetting her own origins, always cultivated and exalted the myth of antique Rome. Never invaded by the Barbarians, she kept the spirit alive in her laws and claimed to be Rome's heir.

Andrea Palladio wrote that, "Venice alone is like a surviving example of the greatness and magnificence of the Romans." Thanks to this continuity one can understand, as Ackerman has demonstrated, how that architectonic form, derived from the primitive Mediterranean house and from Roman and Byzantine villas, found refuge amid the lagoons and contributed to the flowering of the open villa type that enjoyed such success in the Renaissance.

In antiquity, it was Rome that, profiting from its own experience and that of other Mediterranean civilizations, gave the most complex and advanced form to the idea of the villa. In terms of architecture, this became one of the most important Roman conceptions. "If there is a class of building that one can consider the historic expression of Roman society and civilization," writes Mansuelli, "that class is the villa." The very structure of Roman civilization, based on agriculture, favored the development of the villa and the ideals connected with it. The country, through the settlement of the centurions and land reclamation, crossed by an efficient road network linking the various regions of the empire, enjoyed an organization that permitted the villas to extend themselves everywhere.

From the Centurions to the Forest and the Marsh

With the fall of the Roman empire came a progressive weakening of the power of the state and a decentralization of wealth. The decentralization of authority became immediately apparent with the Barbarian invasions. Profound changes in the political order brought about a structural breakdown that led to the collapse of the agrarian systems, to the decay of the great road system, and this displacement of traffic along new arteries. There were also other disastrous consequences. A continuous onslaught of famine and epidemic, following the devastating attacks, resulted in a marked population decrease. The countryside was abandoned. Provincial potentates proliferated; new kings created immense *latifondi* on the borders and governed them with a tyrannical authority unfamiliar to the Roman republic, and even to the empire.

The villas of these new princes increasingly resembled luxurious and well-protected palaces: there arose great porticos where the produce of the fields was gathered; immense courtyards were overlooked by monumental loggias where the lord, surrounded by princely pomp, attended to ceremonies staged in his honor. These buildings would be the ultimate symbolically significant model for all those who in the future aimed to display, through architecture, that power which we may call feudal in substance. Villas of this type can be found in provinces far from Rome. But the example of Piazza Armerina in Sicily serves for all of them. For the complexity of its architecture, it has been compared to Hadrian's villa.

As Mansuelli writes, it became famous because of the mosaic decoration that gave its interior the quality of landscape.

The landscape in this period underwent a profound change. Forest undergrowth and bush invaded the remains of the Roman urban system, the road network, the aqueducts, the temples, villas, and the baths, while marshes submerged lands once parceled out to the centurions. The population lived miserably on the scarce fruits of the earth and by fishing and hunting. Their dwellings were poor huts of straw, thatch, mud, and wattle. Built with local materials, these constructions are the typical functional expression of an economically self-sufficient type of living. The *casoni da valle*, still found in the Veneto lagoons today, are descendents of one of these ancient structures. They have a central empty space, the *portego*, off which open the rooms and the stable. This simple solution, dictated by practical exigencies, lends itself to infinite variations, not only in rural architecture, but also in that of the villa. This was an evolution remarked upon by early theoreticians and even by Palladio.

Towards Feudal Organization: the Castle

The barbarian peoples who invaded the Roman Empire, upsetting the political and social system, brought with them a way of life antithetic to that of the Latin world. Even the changes in architecture demonstrate that. During the Middle Ages in the West and in Italy, the complex Roman agrarian system was replaced by the fief, which was centered around the castle, a tool of war and an

Stone plaque found at Pojana Maggiore (Padua, Archeological Museum).

13

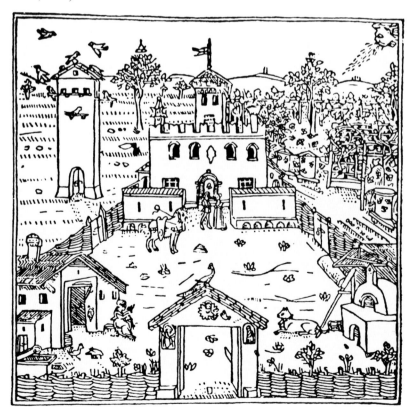

A lady and a knight meet in front of a medieval castle, which had already taken on the function of the villa; a peasant woman spins wool by her cottage; in the background, on the left side, there is a dove-cote, and on the right, the pergola of the kitchen garden (Piero De Crescenzi, De Agricoltura Vulgare, *Venice, 1495).*

instrument of power. Closed and battlemented, the castle reflected the mentality of nordic peoples who, as nomads and warriors, fell upon a society that was based on an obsession with the power of a landed, property economy and then grafted onto it their own ideals of living.

In certain ways, castles seem far removed from the villa and its spirit. The castle is, in fact, an isolated structural complex placed in a defensive position with regard to the outside world, while the villa has an extrovert nature that integrates itself with its surrounding territory, participating in the life of its neighbors, where neither landlord nor peasantry fear siege or invasion.

Notwithstanding these fundamental differences, villas often display characteristics belonging to castles. Like them, many villas exist in a realm of economic self-sufficiency (often in antithesis to the city). Most important, in the villa there survive aristocratic ways of life belonging to the feudal tradition. Even in architectural forms this influence is clear. External elements like moats, walls, towers, and battlements, found in several fifteenth- and sixteenth-century villas and then again in the neo-Gothic revival of the nineteenth century (even if only reduced to a purely symbolic value), testify to a certain continuity between the feudal world of castles and that of the villa. As far as the Veneto is concerned, the intimate relationship with the court of France, that cradle of chivalry and the courtly spirit, must always be kept in mind.

THE RELIGIOUS REORGANIZATION OF THE LAND: THE ABBEY

A new force began to work on the ruined structure of the Roman world; along with feudalism this force exercised its beneficent influence all over Europe.

Western monasticism, especially the Benedictine variety, permeated by the ideal of prayer and work, "*ora et labora*," and heir to the Roman spirit of organization, was committed to both the spiritual and the material redemption of society. Among other things, it promoted reclamation in marshy areas, rehabilitating them for agricultural use. The center of this activity was the abbey, which architecturally could be derived from that closed Roman rural complex called the "*fundus*," which perhaps even more than the castle, contributed some of the most characteristic qualities to the Veneto villa.

There were the abbeys of Nervesa and Follina in the Treviso area; in the Polesine, the abbey of Vangadizza; that of Sant'Illario near Venice; that of Praglia which, in the Padua region, extended its dominion over 5,000 fields.

The abbatial complex was organized around a series of cloisters: an upper area for the monks' recreation, a rustic cloister for country produce, and finally the botanical cloister, where the monks cultivated medicinal plants and fruit trees, thus perpetuating the taste in gardens so popular in antiquity and also conveying cultural concepts prevalent in the near East to the Veneto villa.

The work of the monastics was flanked by that of another religious organization: the military-political orders like the Templars and the Hospitalers of St. John of Jerusalem. Along the remaining traces of Roman roads, usually traversed by pilgrims and merchants, they constructed hospices and hospitals, which were often situated in the same place where ancient "manors" had arisen.

Much later, Venetian nobles and magnates would erect villas on the same sites after acquiring the ownership of these vast holdings.

The importance of the religious authorities, which was not only spiritual but also political and economic, reached its apex when the count-bishops were imperially invested with the administration of vast regions.

The figure of the count-bishop – there are still some examples to be seen in the provinces bordering Austria – appears to incorporate both Latin tradition and feudal authority. But more widespread was the influence exercised in the regional structure, in the life of the individual village, and in mens' minds by the noblest and most brilliant moment in our history: the age of the city-states.

A monk enters the crenelated walls of this abbey: the plants, flowers, and birds show that there was already an interest in nature and in the garden (Fior di Virtù *Venice, 1943*).

The Revaluation of the Individual in the Age of the City-States

The age of the city-states affirmed other ideals, not those ideals belonging to the prince, but those belonging to an extraordinarily new character: the burgher now emancipated from feudal power. Both crafts and commerce – the prevalent urban activities – favored human social contact: they encouraged the acquisition of new techniques; they permitted the development of a political dialectic and contact with more distant lands. In the period of the "Free City-States," structures were created that would be valid in the future.

Next to the centers of religious (the cathedral) and civic power (the town hall), the rapidly developing city saw the proliferation of workshops, factories, and private houses that were usually handsome and often rich, and where the desire for an increasingly comfortable life was always evident. That was clear also in the houses that the rich burghers came to build beyond the town walls; an early expression of the Mediterranean man's instinctual need to live in direct contact with nature, a need that had been institutionalized in the villas of the Romans.

Commonly, in antiquity, it was enough for the prosperous cultured man to have a vineyard in the country. In the first literary evidence of modern villa civilization, we read of a vine trellis or pergola near a fountain; a rose bush or a few fruit trees in the middle of a farm offering a sweet respite in the summer months. Here is the nucleus and heart of our villas. We will search here for that true spirit that the noblest interpreters of villa architecture will renew.

The ideology of the villa, maintaining itself substantially unaltered, developed in such a way that the repetition of phenomena can be verified without having to establish a direct derivation from one to the other.

In that sense the idealogy of Cato and Varro, that working the earth is a purification of the contaminations of the city, are found again in the Veneto, while later on luxury villas became the places of those pleasures that Pliny the Younger described in his letters. This evolution, which was obvious in the provinces of Imperial Rome, was repeated, as Ackerman noted, in the Veneto during the transition from the simple fifteenth-century house to the elegant villas of Palladio.

The first patrons and villa builders did not feel that the villa required forms different from those of the city, adjusted for a new style of living. They repeated in the country the same structures and style of house that they had inhabited within the circle of the town walls, making allowances only for the numbers of family and servants, the private and public functions of the head of the household, and the prestige of the clan.

Venice, the city of merchants par excellence, conserved the bourgeois spirit typical of the era of the city-states. The exigencies of a regime that, even if aristocratic, subdivided its power, taking prosperity into account above all other considerations, continued to be evident in its political as well as social organization, in its customs, and in its arts. This "republican" structure is one of the explanations for the great number of Veneto villas, a trend that culminated in the eighteenth century's "Craze for Holidays," when the possession of a house for vacationing, which elsewhere was the prerogative of a restricted elite, became in Venice and in the Veneto the prize of many, a pale yet significant symbol of a Modern Era teeming with "second houses."

Even when the princes came into power in Italy, Venice retained a municipal organization that was gradually modified by the elasticity of the mercantile mentality that continued to dominate.

The phenomenon of "neo-feudalism" in the Veneto did not encompass only a single family, like the Medici or the Sforza, but a remarkable number of Venetians: in fact all those who had the right to take part in the Maggiore Consiglio.

The extent and especially the longevity of the phenomenon of the Veneto villas is due to these families, to their example and wealth.

Pisanello. Detail from the fresco of St. George and the Princess (Verona, Church of Saint Anastasia, Giusti Chapel). Pisanello and Boiardi interpreted the Renaissance as a return to the world of knights and courtliness.

PRINCES AND THE CULTURE OF THE COURT TAKE OVER

In replacing the city-states, the principalities did not suppress the most vital forces, but instead improved upon many fundamental aspects. Despite the frequent changes in the princes, the continual warfare, and rebellions, it can be said that the character typical of each city and of each territory continued to thrive. Even later, the activities and the traditions that matured in the era of the city-states would always be important.

In this sense each community preserved and perfected attitudes and customs that were reflected in the character of the people, and even in the arts. In each region these were rich in specific attributes and are, therefore, easily recognizable.

Thus we shall see that in Verona, Vicenza, Udine, and other border cities, the principalities encouraged the military arts. Padua, continuing its traditional vocation, increasingly established itself as a capital of culture and science. Treviso cultivated that gay and chivalrous spirit that made it famous. Meanwhile wealth and power tended to concentrate in the hands of a few lords who loved to surround themselves with true and proper courts, set up in splendid royal palaces where an increasingly refined style of life developed, open to the influence of the most advanced European courts.

These customs expressed themselves in art forms characterized by their Gothic source, which, although variously interpreted, was common to all the European courts. Princely pomp expressed itself primarily in works of architecture: in houses, royal palaces, and in castles where their lordships loved to live luxuriously amidst festivities, banquets, and tournaments. They lived surrounded by artists and men of learning who, while exalting the magnificent deeds of their ancestors and ancient heroes, stimulated their ambitions, not only for warfare, but also for the kind of peace where they would be seen as munificent protagonists and the

patrons of true inspiration. In this period great works of reclamation were carried out at Padua, Mantua, Ferrara, and above all at Milan, providing Venice with an example and a stimulus.

The ideals of this courtly world would have profound echoes in the future, especially in the art of Pisanello and in the poetry of Boiardo and Ariosto, while remaining relevant throughout the sixteenth century and becoming models for the Venetian "gentleman."

The villa will be one of the places chosen to show off this aristocratic culture.

PETRARCH AND PRE-HUMANISM AT PADUA

The principalities appreciated the importance that culture could have as a vehicle for fame and as a guarantee of lasting influence. This was confirmed by the spreading study of the Classics, in which it was possible to comprehend the secret of immortal glory.

The new priest of this fame became one of the protagonists of the modern world, the humanist, and Petrarch was the prototype of this new "priesthood." All the great of the epoch fought over him, but he chose to conclude his life in the hills of the Veneto, in that atmosphere of meditation which only the country could offer him. "For me each of the year's seasons offers only throngs of people,

dust, mud, clamour, and rubbish. The country is always amiable and always full of attractions for nobly disposed souls." Crowned poet on the Capitoline, cherished by princes and popes, he found his ideal home at Padua. He had gone there seeking for antique books and desiring to learn Greek, the language that Latin authors held in such high regard.

He realized himself completely in Padua, the city of Titus Livy: ambassador to Venice and counselor to the Da Carrara. He commissioned the painted decoration for the new royal palace. Petrarch created around himself a culture that found a symbolic expression in the three Da Carrara medallions, the first in the modern world to be taken from Roman molds as symbols of a reborn antiquity.

On the hill of Arqua, not far from Abano and Este where Roman remains were continually brought to light and every stone spoke of a venerable antiquity, Francesco Petrarch built himself a house in the country. This was territory pacified by the lords of Padua, the principal artery of the ancients, once trod by Dante, and in an era that had been one of the liveliest centers of the cult of chivalry. There, hermit and priest of humanist culture, he could mediate on the lives of illustrious men and learn ancient wisdom from them.

Near his house at Arqua, Petrarch owned a vineyard, not far from one of those wellsprings that should always be considered fundamental to every human settlement. A little further away opened the valley of Baone, which the poet nostalgically called the "New Vaucluse." Petrarch received his friend Boccaccio at Arqua and, to the end, intent on his studies, closed his life there.

Not only his poetry but his very style of life became a source of imitation. His was a new way of seeing and understanding the country, and Petrarch should be considered the true father of the *World of the Veneto Villas*.

Naturally centuries passed before the idea at the center of our research was accepted: the idea that the architecture appropriate to the villa must be different from that of any other building. But even if the forms of that architecture were still to come, it should be said that the formative spirit of the villa, resurrected from Roman models and writings, was already fully present in the mind of Francesco Petrarch.

Elsewhere, artists and men of letters still lived at princely courts intent on the hunts and the festivities held in royal palaces and castles. However, there would always be one leaving Padua or Verona for Rome in order to measure the columns and monuments with religious care, extracting the secrets of their beauty, and then, like Petrarch, loving the "otio," the idle hours of the classics, retiring to a modest villa to dream of the ancients in blessed solitude.

ANDREA MANTEGNA AND CLASSICAL ART

An iconographic document from the Paduan artist Andrea Mantegna offers us an extremely important starting point for the history of villas in the Veneto. In the background of the fresco showing the so-called "Encounter" in Mantua's *Camera degli Sposi*, just beyond the depiction of the medieval city surrounded by walls and tall towers, between the steep precipices of a hill amid ancient ruins where once an ancient city rose, we see a white marble edifice standing: a classical villa. Through classical texts or rather through antique medallions, frescos, and surviving bas reliefs, Mantegna understood that form of building which Andrea Palladio would know how to revive in his splendid villa architecture a century later.

Mantegna depicts a porticoed edifice with six columns organized on two floors and surmounted by a pediment. It cannot be confused, as might seem the case, with the structure of a temple, but should be understood as one of those suburban villas that Roman nobles, especially in the Imperial period, raised in the city's outskirts for ease of access in their free time, while keeping their utilitarian villas at a distance in more fertile places destined for agriculture.

Based on this knowledge, the few surviving remains of ancient monuments, and on the architectural treatises then available, the new architects sought to satisfy the ambitions of their noble patrons, who had been educated like artists in the ideals of a reborn civilization.

Andrea Mantegna. Detail from the meeting between Marquis Ludovico III of Gonzaga and his son, Cardinal Francesco (Mantua, Palazzo Duvale, Camera degli Sposi). Beyond the city walls Mantegna has portrayed an idealized Roman villa that seems to anticipate the style of the Palladian villas.

The Importance and Influence of Venice

VENICE: CITY OF MERCHANTS

It is typical of the mercantile mentality to extract the best from every experience – to compare, evaluate, select, and acquire. Even before the twelfth century, nothing was done in Venice except importing and hoarding everything that the merchants came across in the course of their voyages that might increase the beauty and prestige of the city's churches and houses. However, the salient aspects of Venetian art can be distinguished in the character of their choices: a great instinct for quality, a taste for refined and precious things, for beauty in the end. But it was above all the spirit of the lagoon and the island that left an impression of unmistakable peculiarities. "The spirit of the waters," wrote H. F. Brown, "free, vigorous, and penetrating passed into the intimate essence of the men who lived on these waters. In the link between a people and its place, Venice manifested the nature of its own personality: a personality so infinitely various, so flexible, and so free."

The responsibility invested in everyone, insofar as everyone there was the "maker of his own fate," was publicly sanctioned in an inscription that can still be read on the exterior of St. Mark's Basilica, near the Porta della Carta that opens into the Doge's Palace: "L'om po far e / die in pensar / E vega quelo che gli po inchontrar" ("A man can do and speak according to his thoughts, and then see what happens to him").

The life of the merchant, with its risks and discomforts, developed invidual and collective capabilities and possibilities, while creating men capable of quick reactions, of prudent decisions, rich in courage and experience, and also rendering them more sensitive to the joys of life, teaching them to appreciate prosperity, decorum, and security. These are ideals that translate themselves into custom as well as into the arts, in architecture, in painting, in a style of living, and in the character of a city.

THE SURVIVAL OF ROME IN VENICE

The great period of the villas in the Veneto would not have been possible had not Venice first prepared the ground on which such an extraordinary culture and art could flourish. The conquest of the terra firma, the work of reclamation, and a political coordination on the part of the Dominante, offered the

The Fondaco dei Turchi (Venice, Grand Canal), as it was before its restoration in the nineteenth century. Also, here the arcades and loggias are reminiscent of those used in the ancient world.

protagonists of this operation that degree of authority, of wealth, and culture that would be interpreted symbolically in the villas erected by Palladio. Only then did the myth of Venice, which claimed to reincarnate that of ancient Rome, find its most significant expression and become disseminated throughout the provinces of the Venetian dominion. Perhaps the way in which Venice kept herself tenaciously bound to the example and the memory of Rome is neither clear enough nor universally known. With her instincts entirely turned to hoarding and with her spirit conservation, she did not limit herself to keeping alive selected laws or forms of government, or to merely inheriting a sense of organization and respect for the state or indeed only continuing the universality of the image of Rome. Rather she made those aspects of Rome's ancient artistic evidence her own as well. It was the villa of the classical world that transmitted its forms to foreign surroundings once the more monumental complexes of ancient Rome had ceased absolutely to be contemporary or relevant. In fact, amid the lagoons, more than in any other place, it seems ancient prototypes survived in the schema of the oldest type of Venetian house.

Thus a city lacking greenery, without agriculture or the support of the countryside, an urban complex completely conceived and constructed by man on the sterile sea, become important, if not determinant, for the continuity and historical development of the villa's cultural and artistic tradition.

This continuity explains how it was that those forms of open architecture, derived from the primitive Mediterranean dwelling and from Roman and Byzantine villas, should find refuge among the lagoons, and contribute to the rebirth of the type of villa that would enjoy such a success in the Renaissance.

THE DOGE SEBASTIANO ZIANI AND THE NEW VENICE: OPEN ARCHITECTURE IS BORN

If there was never a substantial break between the ancient world and the modern world in Venice, that was not an accident. It was a matter of a deliberate choice and a conscious decision that occurred at an easily recognizable moment in its history, thanks to one of Venice's greatest doges: Sebastiano Ziani.

Although Venice's origins are lost in the shadows of the Middle Ages, by the time of the Doge Sebastiano Ziani (September 29, 1172 – April 13, 1178), the city had reached its height in every field. The Maggior Consiglio had been created and the guilds were reorganized. The Rialto bridge was constructed and the Campanile di San Marco erected.

Cesare Vecellio; The Merchant. Degli habiti antichi e moderni di diverse parti del mondo (*Venice, 1590*). *The figure of the merchant has always been fundamental in the history of Venice where profit has always accompanied the philosophy of experience, and the search for pleasure and beauty.*

21

With the Doge's Palace and the squares, the whole of the city's heart was renewed so that it might answer to the republic's new needs and prestige. According to tradition, it was precisely then that Venice was given the right to celebrate its mystical Marriage of the Sea on the Ascension day. The Adriatic was recognized as the true and proper dominion of the Serenissima. The security of this possession had repercussions not only for the Venetians' political conscience. Both town planning and architecture were adjusted to these fresh circumstances, assuming aspects that remained substantially immutable and constant. The character of this architecture (or rather of this new style, linked to a new idea of Venice) reflected a spiritual and political situation already far removed from that of its origins.

But when it was realized that the Venetians' walls and bulwarks were their ships and their fleet's valor, and when it seemed impossible that an enemy could tie up at San Marco, just at that moment the open architecture of the Venetians was born: all porticos and loggias, connected courtyards, windows, and liagò.

When Sebastiano Ziani reconstructed the Ducal Palace, he did not give it the forms of an old-

Jacopo de'Barbari. St. Mark's Square, detail from a plan of the city, 1500 (Venice, Correr Museum).

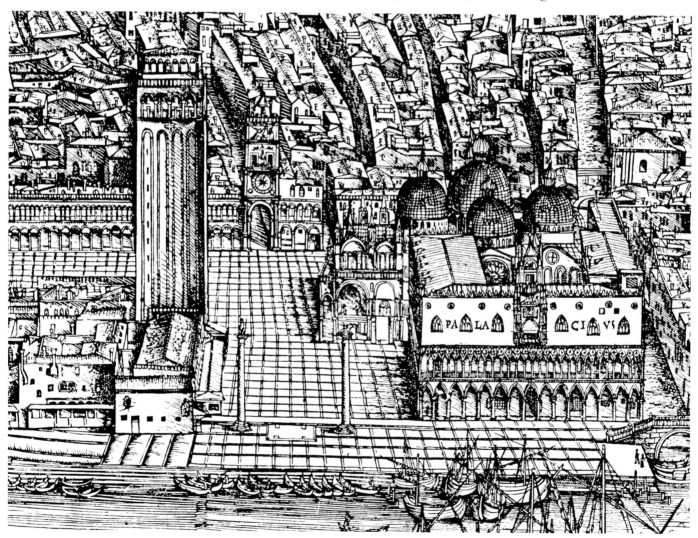

fashioned residence. He wished its structures to be open. He surrounded it with porticos and loggias; he opened its façades toward the lagoon and toward the city. From that point onward Venice would be defended on the high seas, well beyond the Lido sea entrances, far from its holy, inhabited places. There is no barrier between the two columns of the Piazzetta: the gateway leading into the heart of Venice is always open.

Demolishing the fortifications was equivalent to transforming the mentality of the inhabitants. It began with Sebastiano Ziani. Customs and fashions may change, but these happy prerogatives would never be surrendered any more than the psychology and security of those living in a city, unique in Europe for never have been invaded or occupied by an enemy, could ever change. The spirit and the laws of Venice were adjusted to these undeclared and perhaps unclear concepts. The arts adjusted themselves to them, too: the open forms of Venetian design, the "empty center" in paintings; the thousand windows in sumptuous palaces; the open villas of the Veneto countryside. The Venetian experience was also transplanted to the mainland.

Therefore it is logical to think that the type of villa that interests us here – that which tends to fuse interior spaces with the surrounding environ-

ment or rooms and loggias with the landscape (virtually to synthesize man's eternal aspiration to live in contact with nature) – justifies itself best, like the Doge's Palace in Ziani's day, when there exists that particular political and social tranquility such as happened when Venice extended her peace over all the Veneto territory, spreading her ideal of justice and prosperity everywhere.

IDEALS OF WEALTH AND PRESTIGE IN THE HOUSES AND VILLAS OF THE VENETIANS

We have seen how, in the time of the Doge Sebastiano Ziani, a new ideal of life took shape in Venice and how this was manifested in an open architecture that became emblematic of the city and the state.

At the base of the two columns, raised around 1175 by the great doge in the Piazzetta, Nicolò Baratteri sculptured in Istrian stone, eight groups that portray the arts and crafts, the very foundation of Venetian society. Their form was not taken from Byzantine examples. Instead, they reveal clear links with Romanesque art in their realism and with that style that had spread all over Europe from France at the time of the Crusades. Up until then, Venice had turned its interests to civilizations distant in time and space. Only now did it reinforce

Vittore Carpaccio; The Lion of St. Mark (Venice, Doge's Palace). The Lion of St. Mark, coming out of the water and approaching the luxuriant landscape of the Veneto, symbolises the growing interest of Venice in the terra firma.

Part of the façade of Ca' d'Oro, a magnificent example of Venetian Gothic architecture of the fifteenth century (Venice, Grand Canal). The ambitions of the Venetian families and their love of beauty were particularly manifested in the very ornate façades of their palaces.

links with neighboring areas, especially with Verona, a city from which the Venetians supplied themselves with grain, and also with marble for their buildings.

The cultural-political ties with Byzantium were not abandoned, but Venice now opened herself more to the Western world. Often reluctant to accept certain novelties (Giotto's later masterpeices were left in Padua in vain), Venice immediately understood that only by calling to the lagoon specialized workers in the metal and leather goods that were increasingly sought, only by welcoming the masters of silk weaving exiled from other cities, only by imitating the best craftsmen of every nation, could she furnish the European markets with the best products at the lowest price.

All this happened primarily in the fifteenth century, when the city was contributing to an international artistic culture and had assumed a completely new appearance. The florid Gothic seemed most congenial to Venice because it exploited those characteristics of open architecture best suited to the city ever since the epoch of Ziani.

Beyond this, Gothic art corresponded to the need for magnificence, to the taste for decoration, to the love of festivity and ceremonies that constituted another aspect of the Venetian world.

Marble was treated like easy wood; architectonic structures acquired the transparency of crystal, embellished by color and the use of noble materials already employed by the Byzantines and the Arabs. Philippe de Commynes, visiting the city in

1495, remained dazzled by the vision of so many stupendous palaces. "They conducted me along the principal thoroughfare, called the Grand Canal, which is very wide and runs through the city for its entire length... I believe it to be the most beautiful street existing in the world, flanked by the most beautiful buildings. The palaces, built of beautiful stones, are very big and extremely tall. The oldest houses have their façades painted while in this century they dress them with a white stone that comes from Istria, a hundred miles across the sea. Scattered over façades are pieces of porphyry and serpentine marble. Venice is the most triumphant city I ever saw..." The palaces admired by the French ambassador are those that we still see today: the Ducal Palace, just then renovated; the Ca d'Oro; Ca Foscari and hundreds of other "houses" large and small, scattered along the Grand Canal and along the most hidden Venetian canals. This is the moment when architecture excelled over all the other arts. "Among all the languages of the arts of visibility in fifteenth-century Venice," writes Coletti, "Architecture is precisely that one which has the most profoundly original imprint. The architectonic language finds the representative synthesis of practical motives that condition Venetian architecture in its airiness and lightness of structure, a language that the imagination of brilliant artists often succeeds in transfiguring into a noble poetic expression destined to become the small change useful for the most humble utilitarian constructions."

JACOPO DE' BARBARI AND THE PORTRAIT OF THE CITY

In the fifteenth century the city had already assumed a precise appearance. The view engraved by Jacopo de' Barbari in the year 1500 shows us, in fact, a Venice complete in all its parts, a finished and efficient organism. The centers of political and economic power are distinctly recognizable; the various squares are surrounded by the palaces of the principal families and, around these, there are the houses of the "clients." Various activities can be identified, such as those exercised by the guilds in the boatyards, in the arsenal, or even in the warehouses. Various architectural styles are just as recognizable, as is the prevalence of Gothic art.

How precious would be a similar map that, executed with the same diligence and precision at the end of the republic, gave us an overall view of the Veneto provinces with all their towns and all their villas. We could then observe various stylistic changes, as well as the prevalence of the Palladian style. The different functions of the various villas would also be evident: the villas erected as part of a reclamation with their broad surroundings; the pleasure villas; the villas with buildings corresponding to various activities; the villas of the bureaucrats; those of military men, and so on.

Once the city had been formed, particularly at the beginning of the sixteenth century, the Venetians devoted increasing attention to the neighbouring islands of the Giudecca and Murano. There, broad green areas permitted the Venetian merchants to construct buildings and

gardens for discreet meeting with friends. On the Giudecca and Murano, humanists and men of letters could attend to their studies in tranquility far from the gaze of the indiscreet. Jacopo de'Barbari's view is a precious document of this life, where the first Venetian villas in the Gothic or Lombardesque style are clearly visible.

GARDENS AND THE REVALUATION OF THE VENETIAN LIFE

In the Arab world extremely tall walls surround a rectangle of green, in the center of which falls the jet of a fountain-enclosed Islamic paradise, an anticipation of celestial joys. The love of plants and gardens comes from the East. Venetians learned it from their voyages or else by passing part of their lives in lands of Islamic culture.

Doctor Gualtiero was famous for his garden of medicinal herbs in the fourteenth century. Subsequently, botanical treatises and Arab tracts on hydraulics became even more widely known. This

Jacopo de' Barbari; Plan of Venice, 1500 (Venice, Correr Museum). From the thousand palaces of Venice there spread a culture and civilization, of which the villas, too, are a testimony.

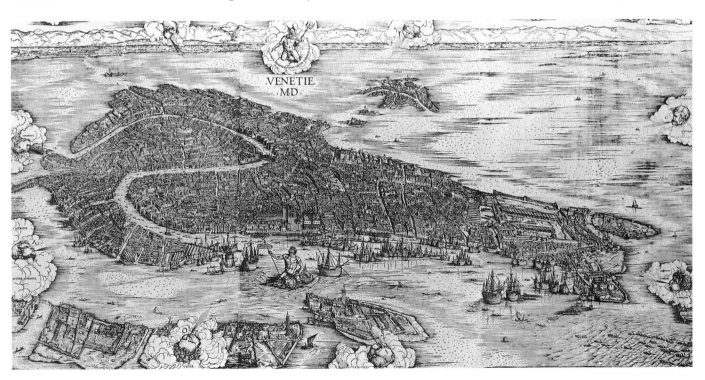

was followed by the introduction of exotic plants to embellish and make the house more comfortable. Venice enjoyed a sort of primacy in Europe in the field of botany. One writer even claimed that there were a larger number of gardens in the lagoons then there were in the rest of Italy.

But beyond the Oriental component, there was another source for the culture of the Venetians and their appreciation of the gifts of life – their links with the courtly customs of France.

Jacopo de' Barbari. A villa on the Giudecca, a detail from the city plan, 1500 (Venice, Correr Museum).

The language (Martino Da Canal wrote the first history of the Venetians in French), music, and the dances of France, along with the poems of chivalry with which Italian literary history begins, all enjoyed great success in Venice. The places celebrated in these poems had characteristics that could not but touch the soul of the Venetians: magic trees and fountains; grottos and valleys of dream and fantasy. In the poems of chivalry, antique mythology returned under another guise with the predominance of the element of fable and enchantment.

The art of the International Gothic (present above all at Treviso, Verona, Udine, and Trento) brought to Venice the echo of delicious landscapes with which to decorate the walls of the Ca d'Oro, painted by Giovanni of France with "gardens and hunting scenes." Pisanello and other artists of the Flamboyant Gothic transmitted the taste for those paradises and the "barchi" that would play so great a role in the Veneto villas.

THE INFLUENCE OF ISLAM AND THE ADRIATIC VILLAS

The villa typical of the Veneto region, open and free on every side, constitutes a step forward compared to the buildings constructed by the Arabs for their pleasure. For example, the Alhambra is crude and inaccessible from the outside. Once we cross its drawbridge and pass through the entrance gate, a series of open spaces stretch in front of us, one after another, free and infinitely interconnected, like being in the interior of a single great house. And all of these places – the fountains, the patios, and the gardens – are accessible and freely offered up for our pleasure.

"I am no longer alone because from here I contemplate a marvelous garden" is inscribed on one of the arches in the Patio of Lindaraja.

If, as far as the exterior is concerned, the Arabs' example has not had any evident influence in the development of the Veneto villas, we should not forget how much Westerners owe to the Arab love of the family and the house, and how much, Venice especially, learned from their wise and lavish use of waters, as well as from their love for plants and gardens.

It is interesting to recall a precedent for the Veneto villas. It did not exist in the lagoon islands or in the mainland territories near Venice, where Gothic and Lombardesque-style villas are extremely rare. We must cast a glance over the territory that belonged to the ancient republic of Ragusa on the other shore of the Adriatic. There we encounter a whole series of Lombardesque and even Gothic villas, still retaining their original forms, scattered amid the green of lush gardens with the white of their handsome stones reflected in the sea or in cool fish ponds. These are not civic palaces, castles, abbeys, or the small houses of the humanists. Here, we can speak of true and proper villas in our sense of the word.

Even if to explain this abundance, we must recall the riches of the Ragusan merchants and their ties with the Muslim world, Onofrio Della Cava must not be forgotten. His aqueduct watered the entire valley. As Praga has shown, there was also lively archaeological activity that, among other things, resulted in a study of epigraphy that anticipated Alberti's own discoveries. So, even in this case, we see villas flourish at the same time as a new wave of reborn antiquity.

The villas of Ragusa, even in their undeniable primacy, should simply be considered as an isolated episode without any great consequences for the future. Neither can they be placed on the same plane as the Veneto villas.

The *World of the Veneto Villas* cannot be the work of a single prince or of a subjugated province as was the case with Vicenta. It needed the Serenissima to realize the vast phenomenon that remained vital, not for a brief period, but until the fall of the republic. In fact, it was Venice, with the unity of its political and economic power, with the solemnity and authority of its principals, and with the prestige of its fame, that succeeded in making a norm of all that elsewhere was sporadic or exceptional. She was always ready to make the most vital experiences her own, no matter where they came from. Venice made over the partial and isolated experiences we have alluded to by using exemplary, organic forms.

THE VENETO VILLA
IN THE FIFTEENTH CENTURY

The stupendous illustrations of the *Poliphilo* give us a clear idea of the gardens where the Venetians liked to retreat to discuss Plato and Petrarch. They were small enclosures with fountains and trellises, embellished with the sarcophagi and sculptures of that classical antiquity which humanism was rediscovering. Nature was experienced in a somewhat literary fashion, even if refuge from the city meant seeking restorative comfort amid the nearest green islands, indicating the importance that the custom of villa life had already assumed in Venice by then.

The gentlemen of the fifteenth century knew that grandiose villas emulating the delights of Baiae had been built, as Martial records, on the nearby mainland and outside the *municipium* of Roman Altino.

That perfectly aristrocratic, completely private pleasure of finding oneself alone with a few friends, is the principal characteristic of these first resorts,

Portal of S. Clement. (Venice, St. Mark's). The refinement of the Arab world has always been an inspiration for Venetian culture.

far removed from sixteenth-century grandeur and the pomp that would distinguish villa life in the last years of the Venetian republic.

From the outset, Venetian architecture was distinguished from that of the mainland by its opening outwards of windows, porticos, and elegant loggias. This style characterizes even the suburban houses, which, still unconnected with agricultural activity, frequently sprang up not far from the city walls.

Indeed the island of Murano seems to have been, from very ancient times, one of the resorts preferred by Venetian noblemen. Among other things they were convinced that the numerous glass furnaces made the air purer.

In the fifteenth century, in the same places where the Venetians had owned mills since the eleventh century, there arose the first suburban villas closed in by orchards and agreeable gardens. The aristocracy "spent blessed hours in the spring and autumn seasons, educating the mind, raising up spirit and body." And here, for more than three centuries, humanists, merchants, navigators, and poets, along with artists and magistrates of the Serenissima, enjoyed the refined pleasures that nature offered.

Benedetto Bordone in 1547 wrote that the island of Murano was "very similar to Venice," but that it offered greater amenities.

The particular humanist atmosphere characterizing these fifteenth-century "resorts" found its highest expression in the fine figure of Andrea Navagero, distinguished man of letters and Venetian diplomat who had a villa with orchards and gardens on Murano.

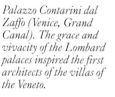

Palazzo Contarini dal Zaffo (Venice, Grand Canal). The grace and vivacity of the Lombard palaces inspired the first architects of the villas of the Veneto.

Notwithstanding the extraordinary abundance of villas that, from the fifteenth to the seventeenth century, made the island into a place of pleasure and amusement, only few traces have come down to us – fleeting clues to a celebrated moment against which the destructive powers of time and men seem aligned. Only Palazzo (it would be better to call it Villa) Da Mula can still offer us tangible evidence of this particular type of villa.

A great number of suburban villas, places for pleasurable and erudite encounters, also rose up on the recently conquered mainland. Despite the centuries of celebration in literature, only slight traces remain of these villas, which were once the setting for refined gatherings and the leisure of the humanists. A common destiny of destruction seems to have overtaken them, preventing us from gathering up that first flowering of the villa civilization in all its richness.

What were the causes? Several ended by being absorbed in the continual growth of urban centers. Once incorporated in the urban fabric, these villas suffered radical modifications that upset their original style. But the greater number of those villas, as we have already hinted and as we shall see more clearly later, owe their disappearance to a precise event linked to strategic and military exigencies – the "Guasto" or Wasting, which Venice ordered in the early sixteenth century in order to clear vast, easily controlled, open plain areas around the walls of the cities. This massive operation, inspired by the need to safeguard the Most Serene Republic, did not spare even the most beautiful fifteenth-century villas in the territory around Padua and Treviso.

If the fifteenth-century villas erected in the open country (and we are thinking, as far as the province of Vicenza is concerned, of the Villa Dal Verme at Agugliaro and of the so-called Ca' Brusà at Lovolo di Lovertino) are excluded, then very few other such humanist residences managed to survive. We are left with too little evidence of one of the culturally, and artistically, most refined moments of Venetian civilization.

Treviso and the Mainland Penetration of the Venetians

De' Barbari's view of Venice, with its representation of the Giudecca and Murano, is precious evidence of a change in Venetian custom of fundamental importance. However, the villas built in the islands of the lagoon were not as yet characterized by the specific architectonic forms corresponding to the new style of living in contact with nature. Even the *villetta* erected in the territory of Padua by Pietro Bembo was little different from a city house. The gardens of these first villas only have a function of pleasure. Their utilitarian function was minimal: perhaps a little fruit, just enough for the family's use, but no more.

The relationship between the building and natural space (which will have a great importance in the Palladian villa) did not require any particular solutions that did not already exist. It was to be on the mainland that new horizons were opened to the Venetians and that the building–natural space relationship will have a determinant value.

The gardens of the houses and convents of the city, the villas of the Giudecca and Murano, are the first stages in a long story, which, almost as if by concentric circles, spreads the Venetians' villa-houses first along the rivers and canals of the neighboring provinces of the mainland (above all in the Treviso province), and then increasingly further away, right up to the borders of the state.

The Veneto villa reaches its definitive physiognomy step by step. Next to the garden, the heart of the villa, is situated everything necessary for agriculture. This is the beginning of a process that was to see many of the best energies of the Venetians directed towards investment in landed property, reclamation, and agriculture.

Treviso was the first mainland territory to submit voluntarily to Venice, and the only one to remain faithful. Indeed we may add that experiments were made in governmental and administrative systems in this province – previously tried in Crete and other colonial possessions in the East – that were then adopted in all the other mainland provinces.

The greatest Venetian families had already begun to appear in the "Trevigiana" by the thirteenth century because of its proximity to the capital. For example, Giacomo Tiepolo had a villa at Marocco in 1289 "where he spent his amusement and where he enjoyed residing." Other similar documents refer to Conegliano, to Nervesa, to Montebelluna, and to Asolo.

Recognizing the benefits that could come from agriculture, it was the Venetian nobles, who themselves had interests in this region, who solicited the government of the Serenissima (they were easy to heed since they often frequented the Doge's Palace) to intervene and coordinate the earliest land reclamation. This was not in the sixteenth century, but rather a century before the creation of the *Magistrato dei Beni Inculti* in 1556. In fact, following requests advanced in 1425 from Castelfranco, the Senate published a decree for reclamation in the province of Treviso with a preface that anticipated almost word

Allegory of the Marca Trevigiana (Cesare Ripa, Icologia, *Siena, 1613). Ripa praises the very agreeable nature of the Veneto, the beauty created by that "great artist, Nature."*

for word the famous pronouncement of Alvise Cornaro: "All holdings will be improved. Many families will transfer themselves there and there will follow an increase in our tax receipts. The harm that was done in earlier times when men and animals were obliged to drink muddy, swirling waters gathered in the ditches will cease with this operation for the conservation of life."

A branch agency of Venice's *Ufficio delle Acque* or Water Board, was formed in Treviso several decades later, in 1469. It coordinated the reorganization of all the Brenta tributaries with "incredible benefit to 59 villas in the area." But that was not all. In the same year a grain warehouse, the *Fontego del grano*, was built in Treviso, a full half century before the famous one built by Andrea Gritti. This was a decision that proved to be one of the Serenissima's most efficacious instruments of propaganda, particularly for the people of the countryside laboring under the nightmare threat of frequent famine.

Reclamation gave new life to the "Trevigiano." It become known as the "garden of Venice," providing a haven for politicians, as well as being preferred by Venetian and foreign humanists. Francesco Barbaro, a disciple of Barzizza and Guarini, sent by Venice as Podestà or Governor of Treviso, already had a villa near Montebelluno in 1411, which he called *Virgilianum* and dedicated in Latin "to a philosophic and tranquil mind."

But even more than the beauty of these places and the fertility of the country, still rich in good water, there was the "securitas" that encouraged the humanists to sojourn there. The consequences of this security guaranteed by Venice was immediately evident, not only in the customs and character of the people, but also in the forms assumed in architecture. Castles and fortifications were no longer necessary and, as has been mentioned, villas make their first appearance with the open forms of their structure.

The *Palazzo dei Giustinian* at Roncade seems to straddle two worlds. The moat, the drawbridge, and the medieval bastions of the castle still seem to protect the villa. On the other hand, the windows, the porticos, and the loggias, along with other arcades and more loggias, frescoed on their outer walls, have the function of accentuating the joy of being able to live in a welcoming and "transparent" architecture safe from every threat.

This is what appears about the new architecture in the *Dream of Poliphilus*, set in the outskirts of Treviso: "The dignity of the construction reconciled a joy and a beautiful grace... What a worthy vestibule, what a regal portico... added to by the dignity of the fenestration... What an admirable order of ornament, and what lastingly fine colors... what well-regulated columns and intervals."

The most harmonious and happy open villa of this period and place is probably that built on the banks of the Sile at Lughignano. It is known incorrectly as the *Villa of Fiammetta*, after the made of Catherine Cornaro mentioned by Bembo. The building certainly reflects the elegance that the Queen of Cyprus, with her humanists and her Greek and Cypriot courtiers, disseminated in a region that Carrer, perhaps following the *Poliphilo*, described as a second "land native to Venus." Cornaro's "Lady Happiness", the "joy of tranquility" recorded by Paruta, the happiness which, according to Carlo Goldoni, is the primary characteristic of the Venetian people – all find their most celebrated models in the lands of the Trevigiana.

The Trevisans' love of festivity culminates in the famous tournaments and with the Castle of Love in 1214. Their emblem seemed to be a classical bas relief of a Bacchante inserted into the wall of the city's cathedral. The elegant paintings of Tommaso da Modena and the happy coloring of Cima da Conegliano are other signs of the courtly and social character of a province celebrated by many Provençal poets of the troubadour and courtly traditions who preferred to frequent this land of the Venetian domain more than any other. Astrological and hermetic research flourished.

Art and Architecture of Venice

Venice and the mainland were two distinct entities during the Middle Ages. One gravitated toward Byzantium, the other belonged to the Holy Roman Empire.

Even during the fifteenth century, despite the fact that Venice had conquered all the Veneto, the Friuli, and eastern Lombardy, there were still marked differences between the lagoon city and the territories conquered by her. The creation of the Mainland Dominion and the aggregation of mainland provinces did not alter, at first, neither Venice's character as a maritime power nor her cultural horizons. Almost a century and the lessons of a lost war, that of Cambrai, would be needed to convince the Serenissima to adopt a unified and organic policy (one which would have the villa as one of its emblems) toward the Mainland Dominion.

First, and one may say for all the fifteenth century, the relationship with the conquered provinces was of an economic character. It obliged Venice to control the rivers and the principal routes of overland communication in order to protect a flourishing traffic with Europe and northern Italy.

Even the cult of humanism that flourished in the nearby cities of Padua and Verona was welcomed quite late in Venice. The Venetian spirit was alien to abstract erudition and remained attached to the concrete realities of practical life, being interested primarily in all that was advantageous to the individual and to the state.

Not that Venice was insensitive to culture. But theirs was still that modeled on examples. The "*Humanae litterae*" of Florentine intellectualism and Paduan archaeological studies remained secondary. Only when Venice began to compete with the most important states of the peninsula did she realize that humanistic culture, already accepted at the principal courts, could be considered an instrument of extraordinary prestige. At first timidly, and then with increasing decisiveness, Venice welcomed the new

forms that art had assumed. Sculptors and architects of the school of the Lombardo family translated the still completely Gothic taste for color, dear to the Venetians, into buildings on a tentatively Renaissance scale. The work of Mauro Coducci was more innovative. He harmonized Florentine architectonic principles – particularly those of Alberti – with the peculiarly Venetian environment, still nostalic for a Byzantine sense of space. Tuscan artists like Andrea de Castagno, Paolo Uccello, and Donatello were called to work in the lagoons; Venice could not be less than other cities. The first villas, in the sense that later became the classic definition for this type of building, had already appeared in Tuscany some decades earlier. For example, there were already present in the *Villa di Poggio a Caiano* many of the elements that would become characteristic, such as the triangular pediment, the colonnaded loggia, and the decoration depicting agrarian deities. This masterpiece of Giuliano da Sangallo reflects the passionate "exhumation" of antique models carried out by Mantegna in the fresco at Mantua and the theorizing on architecture illustrated in the *Poliphilo*.

The architect who had the merit to translate erudition and theory into works of an extraordinary cultural importance was Fra' Giocondo, from Verona. No one was better able than he to understand and use the archaeological learning that had been developed in the Veneto by Tuscan architects.

Coming from a city imbued with classicism as was Verona, that in the late fifteenth century had seen personalities such as that of Guarino, Matteo de' Pasti, Felice Feliciano, and Fracastoro, Fra' Giocondo was not only in a position to absorb the most vital essence of local culture, but also revealed himself to be open to the most advanced experiences of Italian culture. "*Architects prestabilis, nobilis, in architectura omnium facile princeps,*" as Poliziano calls him, Fra' Giocondo is the true protagonist of the relationship between the Veneto and the reborn art of Florence.

A "universal man," as he was defined by Vasari, Fra' Giocondo was second only to Leonardo in the vast extent of his interests.

He ranged from theology to philology from archeology to architecture, and from town planning to painting, distinguishing himself by the clearly scientific character of his researches.

Architecture and reclamation: these two disciplines are the basis for the *World of the Villas* and are the two disciplines of which Fra' Giocondo was the first, great master.

Alvise Cornaro has a description of Fra' Giocondo in his *Trattato delle acque* that alone would establish a man's glory. He asserts that we should "reserve an eternal sense of obligation to the memory of Fra' Giocondo who could rightly call himself the second builder of Venice."

Fra' Giocondo was particularly esteemed as a military architect. For this reason the Serenissima recalled him from France, where the king had named him "deviseur de batiments," in order to bestow on him the high office of official architect of the state. On June 5, 1506 Friuli refers to him as *Fracter Jocundus Veronensis Consilii X maximus architectus*, Fra' Giocondo of Verona, Chief Architect to the Council of Ten. How is it then possible to explain the general lack of interest in Fra' Giocondo? Why is there so much controversy over the works attributed to him? It is strange that even the conception of documented architecture, like the *Fondaco dei Tedeschi*, is not attributed to him.

If we look at the Fondaco's façade and compare it with the central section of the villa erected at Altivole near Asolo for the Queen Catherine Cornaro, we see affinities that confirm Fra' Giocondo's presence in the area around 1507, when he was employed there on the systemization of the Brentella canal and the reclamation of all the territory surrounding the *Barco della Regina di Cipro*.

The great loggia at Altivole introduces us to that most characteristic world of the Veneto villa with its open structure and the presence of elegant columns (both real and *tromp l'oeil*) and with the character of its decoration, where sacred and profane subjects mingle (on one side Apollo and Daphne and on the other Saint Jerome in the Desert) as evidence of the profound relationship between man and nature.

Not only in hydraulic engineering, where the Veronese friar was Alvise Cornaro's master, nor only in military architecture, where he was the master of Sanmicheli and Falconetto, but also in villa architecture, Fra' Giocondo had the opportunity at Altivole, even in calamitous times, to reveal some of the most surprising aspects of his genius.

It is known that Andrea Palladio erected his first colonnaded façade for a villa only in the mid-sixteenth century. Yet we shall see how, especially on the plain of Treviso, villa buildings were erected with grand ground floor loggias and colonnades long before other provinces. The *Loggia di Fra' Giocondo* in Verona is the prototype and symbol of this new chapter in the architecture of the Veneto evident both in the cities as well as in the country. Up to this time, no one has been able to prove that it was the work of Fra' Giocondo (even in this case the documents seem to contradict the attribution). Certainly the loggia reflects the characteristics of a style that recalls Florentine experiences but which, at the same time, seems to correspond to the culture and sensitivity of Fra' Giocondo – that is to that love of ornamentalism that is the halfway between archaeology and the picturesque of the Gothic and the Lombardo family. It is a chapter of history that still awaits an adequate interpretation. The incredibly early date of 1476–91 for such a building in the lands of the Veneto must be taken into consideration.

Fra' Giocondo. Loggia del Consiglio (Verona, Piazza dei Signori). In Fra' Giocondo's architecture, Tuscan dimensions blend with the Venetians' refined taste for decoration.

Giorgione and the Discovery of Landscape

It was not an easy undertaking to distract the Venetians from the vision of sea ports and cities (think of Carpaccio's canvases) that they had always encountered in their voyages. When they thought of the neighboring mainland, they had in mind inaccessible, marshy places, scarcely inhabited by hermits. Reading classical texts or Petrarch's writings was not enough to make them understand and love the country. It was only after Cambrai, when wealth and stability had been reconquered, that we see how the Venetians discovered a nostalgia for the provinces from whence their progenitors had come. The love of gardens, which up to that point Venice reserved for the orchards in the city, partly in association with Eastern countries, and for the villas built on the Giudecca and Murano, gradually extended itself to ever more distant territories of the mainland. Writers and humanists were the first interpreters of this movement, which began with nearby Treviso and had its emblem, even more than in the pages of Bembo's *Asolani*, in the painting of Giorgione.

Considering its treatment of space, the *Tempesta* presents an evolved and complex situation. Michiel's brief description of the painting uses the word "*paesetto*," or small landscape, then notes the meteorological characteristics of a storm and then mentions the characters present.

This scale of interests is not without significance. In the foreground we see depicted a *locus amoenus*, fertile and inviting, outside of time and we would say immersed in nature's eternal breathing. The people who live in the "fabulous" and fortified city that one sees in the background evidently stay away, fearing the ruins of the antique world, not yet overtaken by the wilderness. In fact the two young people, almost symbols of all humanity (and for this reason liable to limitless cultural interpretation), do not take part in the life of the society that belongs to the walled town. They meet in this landscape, selected by the ancients for the construction of a classical villa near a fresh spring. A villa brought to destruction by time and events.

The nature that surrounds the "gypsy" and the "soldier" is generally interpreted as friendly, although neither tidied up nor humanistically ordered as in the gardens of Murano or Asolo, or in those of the *Poliphilo*.

The times were not yet ripe to raise up villa buildings corresponding to the beauties of the place and to the requirements of humanist leisure. But the ideals expressed by Giorgione in the *Tempesta* would not be forgotten by the Venetians when the highest and most complete moment of their villa civilization was reached.

Giorgione; The Tempest (Venice, The Gallery of the Academy). The pleasantness of the secluded position, the presence of water and ancient ruins, seem to suggest the perfect place for the villa of a humanist.

We search to see if among Giorgione's works there is a thread connecting the gradual acceptance on the Venetians' part of that new interpretation of the country that will culminate in a cultural moment still distant, the moment of the *World of the Villas of Palladio*.

The *Fête Champêtre* in the Louvre is one of the most significant and indicative moments in that confidence and harmony that exists between man and nature. It takes place in a land of soft hills, welcoming yet inhabited at last. In this land a group of young people, in full "securitas," comes out of the city visible in the background, happily and humanistically enjoying the consolations of the countryside. In the *Fête Champêtre* we can see the poetic climate fixed emblematically. A climate that, from Bembo and Sannazzaro, goes back to Petrarch and the ancients. But here, as in the *Tempesta*, the presence of the ancient world still has a certain literary taste, and nature is still seen as outside of history in the generic way intended by Bembo's friends: "An earthly paradise for the charm of the airs and the site… Place of nymphs and demigods…," as Calmo will write with his usual artifice.

The other great interpretative moment in the history of landscape will occur several decades later and corresponds to the more mature phase of the *World of the Veneto Villas*. It is a moment that will not be the work of men of letters, artists, or patrons, but of an entire nation of government officials and workers on the land. An admirable moment that neither Giorgione, Sannazzaro, nor Bembo could have either understood or appreciated.

"It cannot be both beautiful and useful," wrote Leonardo da Vinci. However, this was the thinking of those humanists who lived far from politics and reality.

Venice, after Cambrai, will know how to accomplish the miracle. It is true that she will never forget the beautiful (Fra' Giocondo and Alvise Cornaro say so explicitly), but beauty will no longer suffice for the "gentlemen" and in Palladio's villas we shall see the "beautiful" and the "useful" happily united in an admirable whole.

THE NEW ATTITUDE OF VENICE TOWARD THE MAINLAND AFTER CAMBRAI

Between the end of the fifteenth and the beginnings of the sixteenth centuries, events of exceptional importance, such as geographical discoveries, the invention and spread of printing, and the use of firearms, all radically changed European civilization. Venice, a city open to international influence, was ready to welcome novelties and adopt them to increase her prosperity and prestige.

For example, Venice immediately understood the importance of printing to be not only economic, but also cultural and propagandistic, thus giving impetus to the most flourishing publishing industry of the time.

The Serenissima, the most powerful state in the peninsula, favored by economic prosperity, brought a broader political vision to maturity while cherishing the dream of an empire that extended not only over the seas, but also onto the continent.

The expansionist tendency of Venice, which in the fifteenth century had conquered the Friuli and Eastern Lombardy in addition to the Veneto,

Titian; Concerto campestre (Paris, The Louvre). Titian takes up the ideals of Giorgione by depicting the pleasures of villa life.

acquired a renewed vigor at the beginning of the new century, menacing the papal dominions in the Romagna.

Fearful of Venice's increased power and ambitions, many Italian states and with them, Spain, France, and the empire inspired by Pope Julius II, joined together in league at Cambrai (1508) against the republic. They accused Venice of wishing to create a "monarchy similar to that of Rome." The Venetian army was defeated at Agnadello (1509), and the allies penetrated into the territory of the Serenissima reaching the edge of the lagoon. As distinct from other wars fought outside the Venetian state, the war of Cambrai involved the Veneto provinces. Venice, suddenly deprived of financial, military, and food supplies, recognized the impossibility of further recruiting mercenary captains and troops.

The damage that the invading armies inflicted on virtually all the lands of the dominion constituted a fearful ruin for the civilian population and for the very economy of those territories.

Venice, exhausted and bled dry by military expenditure, was in the midst of a commercial crisis at the time of the defeat of Agnadello. Notwithstanding the grave danger, Venice knew how to raise herself up again, thanks to her proverbial diplomatic ability and to a series of lucky circumstances. After alternating military and political episodes, protracted until 1517, the republic was again able to enter into possession of the greater part of her ancient dominion as confirmed by the Treaty of Bruxelles in that same year.

The defeat of Cambrai did not then signify the end of Venice. Indeed, it can be said that hard experience was pregnant with positive consequences. "The Serenissima," wrote Nani, "turned its thoughts to the arts of preservation and peace," which from that moment on were at the top of everyone's thinking, citizens and state alike.

The decadence of levantine commerce, thrown into crisis by the Atlantic routes, by the competition with new fleets, and by the growing Turkish power, convinced many Venetians to invest in landed property on the nearby mainland.

SANMICHELI: FORTIFIED CITIES AND SECURE LANDS

Venice was able to establish more organic investment on the mainland only when her actual possession of it was guaranteed. Prudence counseled that it was not enough to have reconquered the ancient dominion. One had to avoid the repetition of tragic episodes like Cambrai.

At the height of the crisis in 1510, Fra' Giocondo, inventor of "projecting walls for greater safety," was invited by the Republic to equip Treviso with new walls. It was he who, as Vasari again wrote, "first introduced a new manner of making war." Before Sanmicheli's invention, he deserves the credit for having restructured the defense of the Veneto territory. Even the fortress of Legnago was constructed "entirely according to Fra' Giocondo." Operating in the various provinces as architect, hydraulic engineer, and land reclamation official, Fra' Giocondo spread his teaching and his style, furnishing a primary basis for that artistic unification, which, taken up again by Sanmicheli, would culminate with the presence of Palladio everywhere in the region.

The first cities to be fortified were those nearest at hand: Padua and the faithful Treviso.

However, the most important interventions were those of Michele Sanmicheli at Verona. He was a follower of Fra' Giocondo, yet rather than follow the Brunelleschian elegance advocated by the Veronese friar, Sanmicheli was attentive to Roman models present in Verona and Rome (where he worked with Antonio da Sangallo), in order to bring a robust and fervid classicism to the maturity that he would translate in his palaces. Sanmicheli's military architecture was distinguished by the modernness of his solutions. It was he who surrounded Verona with a powerfully bastioned precinct adorned with monumental gates such as the Porta San Giorgio (1515), Porta Nuova (1535), and the Porta Palio begun in 1542. He also erected the Cornaro and Santa Croce bulwarks at Padua.

These grandiose projects assumed an extraordinary importance in the development of techniques and architectonic styles that were common to all the Veneto provinces.

For the construction of these imposing defense-works, conceived and carried out by Sanmicheli, great masses of peasants, bricklayers, and stonecutters were mobilized. Returning to their respective homelands, they retained the master's lessons and helped more or less faithfully to spread his style.

As is evident from the predilection for severe rustication and for the massive appearance of its structures, it was a style born for warfare. It is characteristic of some villas like the Villa Soranza at Treville, built by Sanmicheli himself, and many other of the oldest villas built by anonymous collaborators and scattered throughout the region.

The fortification works of the mainland correspond to the region's political, bureaucratic, and military unification, while favoring the acceptance of a common architectural language.

A similar assertion can be made if we examine the urban reorganization of the cities. In the same years as the fortresses were being constructed, Venice provided for the renovation of squares and public buildings in order to confirm its reestablished domination through architecture.

Jacopo de' Barbari's view demonstrated that Venice was already a completely formed city in all its aspects in 1500. A few years later the Venetians were dedicating themselves with the same industry to the organic systemization of the Mainland Dominion. A centrified force emanating from the Giudecca, Murano, and Treviso now spread over all the region. Taking the capital as a model, the federated cities reproduced its most significant characteristics on a small scale. The symbol of the two columns, the public palace, the loggia, and the clock tower contributed to make them all into many "little Venices."

The *World of the Villas* as a unified and definite phenomenon finds its most characteristic expression only at the outset of the fourth decade of the sixteenth century. However, the year 1517, when the war of Cambrai was concluded and Venice was recognized as lord of all the mainland provinces, had a fundamental and definitive importance for

Michele Sanmicheli. Veronese architect, renowned especially for his military fortifications, Michele Sanmicheli (1484-1559) contributed to the spread of Roman classicism throughout the Veneto. The son of an architect originally from Lombardy, he worked mostly in Verona. Unfortunately, his Villa Soranza, which was the sole example of his work in the Venetian countryside, no longer stands, but his influence on villa architecture is still very evident in the province of Verona.

the new direction taken by Venetian civilization. After that, the cities themselves become responsible for security in the country: controlling and coordinating the territory through the military, the administration, the economy, and culture. A new aristocracy emerged from those cities and from their organization of power, giving birth to a greater flowering of feudalism in a country that was, in turn, controlled with an apposite magistracy by Venice. Thus all the lands of the mainland assume their role and significance within the pacified and reorganized region.

Only keeping this in mind can one explain why the open architecture of the Veneto villas, instead of the fortification of castles, proliferated in the plains, on the hillsides, and along the rivers.

Only after 1517 did the Veneto province begin to acquire its own distinct physiognomy or appearance, reflecting that of the Serenissima, but also recalling a world apart from Venice: neither commercial nor bourgeois, but essentially of the peasantry. The happiest results from this osmosis come when local cultures embrace a Venetian

Jacopo Tintoretto; Portrait of Alvise Cornaro (Florence, Pitti Palace).

ALVISE CORNARO AND THE GENERATION OF THE "FOUNDING FATHERS"

These problems were at the center of the thinking of Alvise Cornaro. His teaching emphasized land reclamation and "holy agriculture" as the way to stimulate Venice. This was accepted with enthusiasm by the many rich "provincials" who constituted the base of a way of life, no longer tied to the sea and trade, but rather to the land and agriculture.

The capital regarded the mainland with increasing interest because of the mainland's own original contributions. Cornaro became the most important spokesman of this new interest. At first his solutions met with indifference, incomprehension, and opposition from the most conservative Venetians, yet it was thanks to Cornaro that the "Venetian capital was invested in the acquisition of landed property and sundry reclamation projects," becoming the foundation for future stability.

Cornaro's example and urgings finally led the Serenissima to establish that *Magistrato sopra I beni inculti*, which was the basis of the Venetians' new political economy. It also represented the decisive and most representative period for understanding the true significance, the basis, and the timeless success of the Veneto villas.

Cornaro had learned from his family's experience with commercial failure that, despite his own claims to the most illustrious Venetian noble descent, it was not at sea, but in agriculture that prosperity and the future of the state should be sought. Once he had made himself rich, Cornaro sought and found the support and, in a manner of speaking, the ideal justification for the excellent results of his own personal experience in the classical culture that had always had one of its principal bastions in Padua. "The accepted practice that recognized agriculture as the sole legitimate and honorable activity for a free man," seemed valid to Cornaro as well.

The solidity and extent of his interests were a part of the nature of his Paduan surroundings where an open and pragmatic spirit viewed the University as the center of the most advanced

have been born. Experience derived from contact with modern reclamation projects in Lombardy was spread over all the Veneto by Brescian technicians, especially after the sacking of their city by the armies of the League of Cambrai in 1511. At Treville Sanmicheli erected the Villa Soranza, one of the first modern villas in the region. In the Veneto, however, the problem of reclamation was very complex. There was need to free the mainland countryside from marshes by channeling the waters into *retratti* in order to make them flow smoothly to the sea.

studies. There, where Copernicus had studied and where the unprejudiced teaching of Pietro Pomponazzi was welcomed, scientific research developed freely (freedom of investigation was guaranteed by the laws of the Serenissima), culminating in the new scienctific anatomy studies of Andrea Vesalio.

But Fra' Giocondo could also be Cornaro's true master. Like him, Cornaro combined the competence of an hydraulic engineer and reclamation expert with a talent for the arts, which made him one of the principal protagonists of the history of architecture in Veneto. Cornaro had derived from Verona (particularly through Fra' Giocondo's teaching) the sense of a serene and balanced architecture, otherwise quite exceptional in the Veneto. And from Verona he wished to take the architect Gian Maria Falconetto to Padua as a collaborator in the building projects that he was planning for his properties. As a writer and patron, Cornaro loved to surround himself with "men of fine intellect," forming that which could be considered a true "Academy."

The meetings directed by Cornaro certainly gave primary importance to the best and most worthy means for solving problems connected with agriculture, building, and decoration. Arcadia, with its choruses of satyrs and nymphs, was somewhat out of place in such a passionate and vital atmosphere. Trissino and Serlio, with all their utopias and culture, seem anaemic in comparison with Alvise's concrete vision. However, such was not the case with Palladio who in his "Books" on architecture seems to have given substance to Cornaro's ideals.

It was precisely Cornaro's friends who favored Palladio's work. They were the contemporaries of the great architect and fathers of those noble patrons who intended to interpret, with the creation of their villas, the ideals of their parents as founder of the family. We read in the *Four Books of Architecture* that many of the villas, such as those at Montagnana, Campiglia, and Quinto Vicentino, for example, were made not for the present owner, but after the explicit desire of his father, one of those noble friends of whom Alvise Cornaro

spoke: agriculturalists, men of letters, and even architects, splendid "dilettantes."

Alvise Cornaro's social conscience – as self-interested as it may have been – was always of decisive importances clothing his works with ethical and religious significance.

Even though Alvise Cornaro took inspiration from Rome in external appearances and in the spirit of organization and the nobility of his enterprises, it was through a Christian spirit that he conveyed a concept of communal life quite different from that of antiquity. The Veneto "gentleman" considered his peasants in a familiar way as distinct from the Roman of the *latifonda*, participating with them in the principal events that marked life in the villa during the year.

Angelo Beolco, called Ruzante, was a valuable witness to many aspects of this situation. "A man who perpetrates a villainy is not someone who lives in a villa, but rather a villain," said one of his characters, paraphrasing Cornaro in *Reduce*.

The old antagonism between the city and the country seemed to enjoy a truce at this time. Indeed, the most interesting aspect of Ruzante's great innovation was that the country was not presented to us from the landlord's point of view by the extraordinary Paduan writer, as is the case in almost all the other historical and literary sources that we know, but from below, specifically from the point of view of the peasants who lived in the same environment where the villas are born. Naturally Beolco speaks of Alvise Cornaro, his friends, and their ideals of villa life with great respect. "I shall tell you. Those are called good men who, according to their rank and talents, know how to dispense their goodness honorably; who have increased rather than diminished their talents; and who take pleasure in building and bringing valleys and woods under cultivation. They have enough friends to give them aid when they are in need. They favor the virtuous of every class and condition. Above all they are happy men and *not melancholic*." However, the enthusiasms of Cornaro and his friends were also reflected in the peasants' way of thinking and in their concept of life.

However, socioeconomic programs and ethical commitment were not the only forces to guide and sustain Cornaro and his partners. An outspoken aesthetic criteria directed their every move, be it in their lives as gentlemen who intended to live in a dignified fashion, or in the works conceived and promoted by them as a reflection of, and testimony to their very ideals.

The reclamation projects carried out by Cornaro, at least as far as he himself specified, had the merit of making areas of marshland "once ugly, beautiful."

Like the most worthy men of antiquity, Cornaro asked of life all the joys that it could offer. For this reason, he enjoyed his "suburban villa" located near the Basilica del Santo at Padua, his utilitarian one built in the middle of his farmland at Codevigo, and that one reserved for "relaxation" and for hunting, situated amid Este's pleasant hills.

While today we can still admire the Paduan buildings, the Loggia and the Odeon, as conspicuous examples of the most balanced teaching of contemporary Roman architectonic culture, there remains of the Este villa only a harmonious and refined triumphal arch known as the *Arco Benvenuti*. But among all the buildings erected by Cornaro, it is the complex at Codevigo that more than any other merits the term "villa" in the sense that we recognize today as applicable to the Veneto villas. With the landlord's house as its center, composition was appropriate to agriculture.

Cornaro's example became emblematic as far as the world of life in the villas was concerned. "I pass my time," he wrote, "in the greatest delight and pleasure at all hours because I find I frequently have the opportunity to converse with honored gentlemen, with men of great intellect, men of fine manners, and of letters: excelling in every virtue. And when I do not have their conversation, I set myself to reading some good book. And when I have read enough, I write. In all this I seek to please others to the limits of my abilities.

"All these things I do in their own good time and in greatest comfort in my rooms, which are located in the best neighborhood of this noble and learned city of Padua. I built them on the principles of architecture which teach us how it should be done. Beyond this I take pleasure in my various gardens and with the running waters that flow nearby. I always find something there to delight me.

"I have yet another means of relaxation to which I resort in April and May and also in September and October. For several days at a time I enjoy a hill of mine situated in the most beautiful part of the Euganean hills. There are springs and gardens and above all a fine and comfortable room where I relax after the easy and pleasant hunting I permit myself at my age. I delight in my villa on the plain for just as many days. It is beautified by the number of handsome streets which meet in a fine square with a church in the middle. Given the possibilities of the place, it is a well-maintained building. The beauty of the location is also enhanced by a broad and fast-flowing stretch of the Brenta river which divides the property. The large areas of land on either side are fertile with well-cultivated fields."

Beyond his merits as a hydraulic engineer, as a writer, as a patron, and architect, that which best defines Alvise Cornaro's character and his social and historic importance was his idea for a *Magistrato dei beni inculti*. It is for this that he may be considered the founder of the *World of the Veneto Villas*. He did not limit his experience to the private sector, but through his political activities he made himself the link between the state and individual proprietors, between the capital and the mainland. According to the typically Venetian spirit that Alvise Cornaro personified, individual initiative should be accompanied by a collective, integral commitment, leading to a central coordination and working to help rationalize the structure of the region.

It was Alvise Cornaro, acting as a private individual, who urged the Serenissima to pledge a commitment to land reclamation and the agricultural improvement of the whole Veneto territory. "Of 800,000 *campi* in the districts of Treviso, Padua, Verona, and the Polesine," he wrote bitterly, "200,000 are marshland." And he concludes:

"The *Signoria* has the obligation to transform its lands from the ugly into the beautiful, from a melancholy aspect to a good and healthy, and from fallow to cultivated."

It was primarily thanks to him that in 1556 the republic created that magistracy that undertook all the reclamation work, giving the region an appearance that distinguished it from all others.

RECLAMATION AND THE *MAGISTRATO AI BENI INCULTI*

Following the *Terminazione del Magistrato dei beni inculti* (or the "Termination of the Magistracy of Uncultivated Properties") of June 30, 1563 and the publication of the *Piano generale per la sistemazione e regolarizzaxione di tutte le acque scorrenti fra I Colli Berici e gli Euganei* (or the "General plan for the ordering and regulation of all the waters flowing between the Berican Hills and the Euganean Hills"), provision was made for as many consortia as there were rivers to control. An overall integral plan, based on the altimetry of the territory, coordinated the flow of the rivers, the drainage of ditches, and the irrigation of land endangered by drought. With a complicated and complex system of sluice gates, dykes, and raised beds, the waters began to follow a course determined by man. The marshes were dried while dry lands were furnished with the water necessary to guarantee constant harvests.

To have an idea of the spirit in which the Venetians set about the great works of reclamation, we read in the *Parti prese dall'eccellentissimo Senato in materie de' beni inculti* (the "Senate debates on the subject of uncultivated lands") report number 21: "That in the Moncelese network the procedure should be of three orders in imitation of our Lord God who, in the making of the world, first divided the skies from chaos, then separated the land from the water, and finally had the earth give birth to specific things: animals, trees, and grain. Thus each network can be completed in three stages. The first, bringing the waters up out of the earth..."

Hydraulic machine (Fra' Giocondo, M. Vitruvius, per Iocundom solito castigatior factus cum figuris et tabula ut iam legi et intellegi possit, Venice 1511).

There was an ever increasing amount of the land available for agriculture thanks to reclamation. This was constantly improved through the introduction and increased production of new crops, such as corn and mulberry trees, and the adoption of systems of crop rotation that provided for a more rational exploitation of the soil.

Industrial activities were strengthened, favoring the manufacturing specialities of each territory – arms at Brescia, textile working and silver at Vicenza, silk in the Friuli, hemp in the Verona area, and wool at Padua, as can be seen in the allegories of each province that artists painted for the public palaces of the capital and the state. Political functions, craft workmanship, and industry are reflected in the types and the location of buildings, each of which reveals its significance through the choice and application of structural and decorative elements.

A new city was born, the *City of the Villas*. Just as the deserted beaches of the lagoon were populated with ever grander and prouder buildings, so the desert land of the mainland, reclaimed and brought under cultivation, was peppered with villas. In a short time the whole of the Veneto assumed the aspect of a marvelous organism, with stupendous buildings like royal palaces, placed in the center of vast farmlands.

Andrea Palladio – an Outstanding Architect

PALLADIO

Many of the characteristics typical of the villa world were already defined by Cornaro's day, but only with Palladio did these reach full maturity. Despite representing the noble forms of classicism, the villas of Cornaro, Sanmicheli, and Sansovino were singular, isolated episodes. Palladio's villas, on the other hand, summarized and spiritually elevated all the multiple and complex components considered up to now, translating ancient and modern aspirations and ideals into urbaned and architectonic terms.

They interpreted the peculiarities of the site and the patron's requirements with an absolute equilibrium, without diminishing their fundamental and unmistakable stylistic and poetic unity. Because these villas taken together were the expression of a great and complex movement, they seemed to share uniform characteristics throughout the vast territory. They were no longer "exceptions," but models that could be realized and exported outside the Veneto, and even outside Italy.

The work of Palladio, the definitive consummation of all the preceding periods, was built on a substratum of political and economic factors as well as social and cultural considerations. But whoever judges Palladio's lesson solely in terms of his architectural proportions and forms – the erudite abstractions of a brilliant architect – and sees them solely as models of absolute beauty, has not taken into account that these buildings, removed from the natural context for which they were created, would seem dried up and deprived of the roots that tie them deeply and inextricably to the climate, the landscape, and the history of the place. As Ackerman observed, only those who have never visited the Veneto can reduce Palladio in the formule of the classicists to the role of theorist in the *Four Books of Architecture*. Palladio was also "a magician of light and color, the Veronese of architecture."

It was precisely "this synthesis of sensual and intellectual elements" that explains the success of Palladio's genius in different countries and epochs, even though the eighteenth-century purist reaction attempted to fix him within their rigid scheme of eternal law.

In addition one can not underestimate the fact that Palladio's villas rendered concretely the ideals of an epoch important for the West. In one of the most significant aspects of Palladio's vision of the world, the villa seems to be the complete expression of the Renaissance. The Veneto villa represented the arrival of a revolution that had put an end to a medieval concept of the significance of man's life. Christianity had preached scorn for the gifts of life for centuries. It had taught men to value each thing with regard for its moral value and to consider the entire universe exclusively in relation to religion, thus minimizing the works and aspirations of man. The permissible artistic creations were collective works (cathedrals, municipal palaces), more than the work of single artists. Their function was that of exalting God or else the social structure considered as a divine emination.

In the people's imagination the forests, the springs, and the country were all populated with malignant spirits who haunted classical ruins, the surviving testimony of pagan antiquity. Even though they loved antiquity passionately during the humanist movement, men regarded it as an inimitable, remote Golden Age.

Without wishing to follow a rigid scheme inapplicable to Palladio's work, one can describe a division of architectonic types that takes the patrons into consideration. Thus "the villas in the first, unadorned style, lacking columned porticos," such as the Villa Godi at Lonedo, were constructed for Vicentine noblemen, while the villas formed of a two-story block, like the Malcontenta, and that with a single floor with long wings, like the Villa Badoer at Fratta Polestine, were ordered by Venetian nobles.

In the same way, the Rotonda was repeated at Meledo for the Trissino, who were also Vicentine patrons, while the Villa Serego, which remains unique in Palladio's œuvre, is evidently linked to the culture of the Veronese noblemen who commissioned it.

With respect to the first villas that the humanists erected among the gardens of the Giudecca and Murano or along the rivers of the Treviso province, the Venetian "gentleman" did not think solely of the beauty of these "terrestrial paradises" idealized by the Petrarchan tradition. Fantasy and fortune, consciousness of history and the virtues, all converged to create a new interpretation of the world. The "total vision" that existed in Palladio's villas combined "beauty" and "utility" in harmonic symbiosis, thus superseding Leonardo's memorable judgement. It is precisely this solidity that freed Palladio from rigid classicism. The first years of his life were particularly important in this regard. The origins of Andrea di Pietro della Gondola were rather humble. Even his artistic training was of a modest and essentially practical character, taking place in stonecutters' workshops, first in Padua and then in Vicenza.

In *The Four Books of Architecture* he illustrated his architectonic undertakings while at the same time extolling his patrons. Conscious of their dignity, he offered them a way to glorify themselves. "And why it is convenient that one should say something about that which will be consonant with the quality of him who will inherit. Its parts should correspond to the whole and to each other. But above all the architect should take warning (as Vittruvius says in his first and sixth book) that grand gentlemen, the greatest of the republic, will require houses with loggias and spacious and ornate rooms so that they can entertain those who await the master to greet him or beg some help or favor. For lesser gentlemen, lesser buildings are seemly, costing less and with fewer adornments. For lawyers and advocates one should build in such a way that their houses have pleasant, decorated places to walk in so that clients may remain there without tedium. The houses of merchants should have places facing the north where merchandise can be stored in such a way that the landlord need not fear burglars."

We can already see, in these phrases of Palladio, the distinctions drawn between various types of patrons, distinctions that correspond to various types of villa to be built.

Andrea della Gondola, Gian Giorgio Trissino's favorite and protégé, found the perfect atmosphere for his training in Vicenza. It was there that, ennobled even in name as Palladio, he made his official entry into the most refined society.

Andrea Palladio, Frontispiece of I Quattro Libri dell'Architettura *(Venice 1570).*

To satisfy the requirements of the Vicentine families, Andrea Palladio constructed palaces in the city and villas scattered in a countryside that, not long before, had been rich in towers and castles. The souvenirs of these were revived in the prestige of Palladio's art forms. The artist did not remain entrapped in Trissino's narrow circle but, increasing the number of his patrons, gave a vast scope and new possibilities of expression to his art in a series of directions that extend from the Villa Cricoli to the Rotonda.

He also made himself into the spokesman of that Roman spirit that pervaded the "myth of Venice," as well as the heroic ideal of the Renaissance.

The artist was formed first as a "modern" man and he approached architecture, associating himself with the ancient world, not in order to reflect it like a mirror, but to capture the spirit and apply it in a "modern" way. Palladio traced that vaguely anthropomorphic hierarchy of parts that inspired his architecture back to antiquity. Thus the central part "corresponds to the head and to the torso of the human body, while the axis of symmetry corresponds to the spine." In the villas this hierarchy established the predominance of the residential building over the wings of the *barchesse* or outbuildings. A more elegant Ionic order was chosen for the principal architecture while the Tuscan order usually characterized the other. But

organic nature was not discernable in Roman houses and villas. The Romans used free plans for private dwellings. In fact Palladio was able to find the inspiration for his dream of classicism only in public buildings and especially in the Imperial baths. Palladio sketched Roman ruins with great fidelity on the spot, while in his studio he "reconstituted them into a rigorously Palladian scheme" following the three rules recorded by Ackerman: hierarchy; integration of the parts through proportion; and the coordination of the interiors with the exterior through the projection of the internal form onto the façade.

The antique world was not, for Palladio, a model from which to take various architectural motifs, but rather an ideal in which the new "religion" of his era could be recognized. His architecture was permeated with this ideal, which he brought into existence with the spirit of a true "demiurge."

It was only natural that his gifts revealed themselves particularly in villa architecture, where spaces were more ample and free. Palladio designed like an urban planner. "The city is nothing more than a particular enormous house, while a house is a small city." Thus, in contrast to the architects of the early Renaissance who designed for aggregation rather than integration, he conceived of the entire villa building with its various functions of the useful and the beautiful as an organic entity, closely linked with nature, seen both as a landscape setting and as agricultural land.

All of this was supported by laws of harmony, according to the proportional relationship that extended into the third dimension and that can be considered "harmonic" in a narrow sense, associated with musical theory. Palladio's naturalism was rationalism, a research carried out in the laws that regulate life, as distinct from Michelangelo's naturalism, which was rigorously biomorphic and also alien to mathematical abstractions and, as Ackerman observed, where architecture was understood virtually as a living body. It was precisely this rational and abstract aspect of his work that was the source of his success in nordic countries. On the other hand, the fact of his having been trained in the "stonecutter's craft," and having tasted and experienced every sort of material, never hurt his art but rather prevented him from becoming excessively abstract. His working methods and the healthy relationship that he enjoyed with his collaborators and with his best foremen also certainly benefited.

Thus, if on the one hand Palladio's architecture was the expression of pure relationships, in another way it was concrete work that can be appreciated almost like sculpture.

Palladio derived his linearism from remote and subtle Byzantine and Gothic influences, typical of the Veneto traditions, the same influences that Mauro Codussi knew how to transform into harmonious spaces and Renaissance forms. Palladio did not align himself with the Flamboyant Gothic and its festive decoratism or polychromy; his was the line that cut through pure space.

Palladio neglected no stimulus, no suggestion, no historic psychological or literary factor needed, to bring his vision to maturity. He welcomed points of departure like castles or "casoni," huts or other agrarian structures. He learned from Vitruvius, Bramante, Serlio, Alberti, Sansovino, Cornaro, and from Roman ruins – especially those in Vicenza such as the Berga theater.

On his travels to Rome he was continually stimulated by the antique monuments that he measured endlessly, as he did those buildings designed by Bramante, Raphael, and Michelangelo. Nonetheless his personality remained independent and autonomous. Thus in his works, he offered a new and concrete point of reference to the architecture of the time with forms that would be recapitulated and would have a vast distribution because they had been humanized in the Veneto fashion.

No one has known how to offer man more dignified dwellings better than he. These men were not just invested with political power but were like demigods at the acme of the heroic ideal, rulers of their world and of life. Palladio made their myth concrete and became the intermediary for an ideal that has stimulated men for centuries. These ambitious dwellings were not, however, interpreted by

Andrea Palladio. Detail from the interior of the Pantheon (I Quattro Libri dell'Architettura, *Venice 1570).*

the artist in a disproportionate fashion. His villas are never too "aulic." They adapted themselves almost naturally to their environment and to their functions. Even though they were magnificent, they belonged to a wholly Venetian scale. This is because Palladio intended the villa to be a beauty that gave pleasure, like health and the respect for mankind, like profit and work for all, or like nature and art: art as the symbol of man's domination of nature.

The teachings of Venice and its exemplary history were often used as a model by other nations that hoped to achieve the immortality to which the Republic of St. Mark seemed destined.

The rediscovery and appreciation of the Veneto landscape, begun at the beginning of the sixteenth century in Giorgione's painting, also found affirmation in another mainland artist, Andrea Palladio. In the one as in the other, we can witness the realization of a miracle of harmony that is born of the most varied experiences but that also has the unmistakable fascination of an extraordinary freshness.

The Villa Barbaro at Maser and the Ideal of Harmony

The concepts that guided the brilliant Palladian intuition in the realization of the villa at Maser, were an ideal of superior harmony, a refined humanistic culture, and a profound link with the natural environment.

The selection of the site was significant above all. The bond between the edifice and its surroundings surpassed the choreography outside of trees and lawns, and took root deep in the land from which the "Maser spring" emerged, ceding its name to the villa. This spring, rich in symbolic interpretation, acted as the go-between in an ideal marriage between the human, earthy element and the sky. It became the protagonist of the humanist dream that the Barbaro brothers, refined cultivators of antiquity, transmitted to Palladio.

Palladio was a profound student of classical architecture, partly thanks to his collaboration with Daniele Barbaro on the illustration and publication of Vitruvius, and he undoubtedly sought to interpret the models of antiquity in a modern key. The villa at Maser lent itself wonderfully to his project. The Palladian building extended horizontally half-way down the slope, opening onto the green Treviso countryside, almost repeating the gentle rolling of the hills. From the decisively projecting central block, crowned with a classical pediment, stretched two long arcaded wings culminating in picturesque dovecoates. For his noble Venetian patrons, Palladio fused architecture in which the residential buildings and those destined for agriculture, while the entire villa "inserted truly into the country, cordially opens toward its surroundings." The Barbaro were certainly not country folk, but were distinct from Roman nobles closed up in their palaces. Venice's

Andrea Palladio; Villa Barbaro at Maser.

aristocratic families had made their fortune in maritime commerce, and this had given their culture a sense of the practical that was maintained even in their humanistic studies.

This is perhaps one of the keys for understanding the "poverty" of Palladian material. While the patron's residence bestowed nobility on the outbuildings which, even though they were hierarchically inferior, were an integral part of the villa, at the same time these rustic additions seemed to transmit their essential simplicity to the main building.

Palladio thus became the greatest interpreter of Veneto culture in the classical mode. And in this sense, it is opportune to recall what Ackermann observed: that Palladio was the first to discover "the unadorned style of the ancients," the buildings that had been built by engineers like the exterior of the Pantheon or the Baths, which were bare of any decoration.

The central square hall of the villa was the fundamental nucleus of the building, an almost sacred place that provided, in perfect harmony with the patron's ideals, the setting for Paolo Veronese's fresco of *Olympus*. From this room there was direct access to a raised level outside where the Nyphaeum appeared, emerging from the thick vegetation that surrounds the villa. The atmosphere of this area, where the sacred fount of Maser was celebrated, was a profound one. From here burst the jet of perpetual waters that fed and enlivened the place.

The Barbaro's residence is universally famous for the vast cycle of frescos carried out by Paolo Veronese. Critics have frequently put forward the hypothesis that there had been a disagreement between the painter, whose name is never mentioned in the *Quattro Libri*, and the architect. Yet no other artist could have animated these rooms with figures, decorations, and perspectives so perfectly in harmony with the purity and nobility of the Palladian architecture. Climate, landscape, nature, and human activity all seem wonderfully intertwined and fused together in this villa, one of the highest poetical peaks of Palladian art.

Paolo Veronese; Portrait of a cellist, symbol of Harmony (Maser, Villa Barbaro).

ANDREA PALLADIO AND NOBLE PATRONAGE IN THE BASSO VICENTINO

An effective understanding of Palladian buildings cannot ignore a direct, firsthand experience of the sites or an analysis of the territory's historic and geographic characteristics. Only in his conception of the Villa Trissino at Meledo, the architect, strongly influenced by the boundless ambition of that noble Vicentine family, ended by proposing an absolutely impossible project that did not even take the topography of the site into account. Inspired by the Acropolis-like complexes of the Roman world, disposed on various levels linked by majestic staircases like the Temple of the *Dea Fortuna* at Preneste, the Villa dei Trissino could never have been adapted to the site at Meledo, which was situated on a tiny hill only a few yards high.

However, for Palladio, this was rather an isolated case. Generally the Vicentine architect gave great attention to the characteristics of the site in order to exploit what nature offered him. At this point it is opportune to observe how the villas that interest

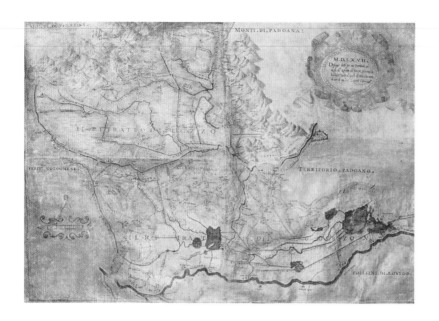

Domenico de Rossi. Map of the territory surrounding Gorzon, Brancaglia, and Lozzo, and also of Monselice, taken from an earlier one by Luca Zappati, 1567 (Venice, Correr Museum). From very early on Venice had invested its officials with substantial means and authority to regulate the rivers and reclaim the land in the region.

us almost all grew up in the area included in a map drawn up in 1567 to show the enormous reclamation project known as the *Retratto di Lozzo*. The Basso Vicentino constituted a point of confluence for various water courses (coming from the territories of Verona and Padua), which created marshland and made thousands of acres unsuitable for cultivation. This unfortunate situation in the three Basso areas obliged them to fight constantly against the waters. The intervention of the Venetians resolved this in the first half of the sixteenth century, when the marshes were drained and the rivers that had flowed freely and uncontrolled were redirected back into their beds. Similar to Venice, in the territory of Vicenza the country would not have the appearance that it has today without the prescence of the nobility. An agricultural vocation and specialized production in certain sectors led to the presence of these patricians in the sixteenth century. The peaceful coexistence of the noble with the peasant was an interesting and very special phenomenon in the Vicentino. The relations between the Repeta family and the community of Campiglia dei Berici document this reality.

The Repeta as feudal lords presided over the

sittings of the local council and when it came to putting highways in order, draining marshes, defending the village in difficult legal quarrels, or providing both doctors and medicines during epidemics, these local lords undertook to meet all the needs of the population.

The same was true for the church and for other public buildings. *The World of the Veneto Villas* was characterized by a particular modus vivendi: by an osmosis between the noble patrons and the local population. The townsman mentality of the villa builders conditioned the life and mentality of the country folk.

Our itinerary could begin with the Rotonda situated in the immediate outskirts of Vicenza a short distance from Bacchiglione, a navigable river famous for having been used by the Vicentines for flooding the city of Padua. Only after the systemization of the Bisatto Canal did the Riviera Berica, no longer menaced by flood waters, acquire many inhabited settlements and villas. The patron of the Rotonda, Paolo Almerico, a "man of the Church" as Palladio described him, had been nominated "Apostolic Referendary" during the papacies of Pius IV and Pius V, and by virtue of his merits had become Roman citizen. Having enriched himself, he returned to his homeland, where he increased his prestige by having Palladio build his suburban villa. Almerico collected rents from different parts of the Vicentine territory including the church at Lumignano. With Almerico, Palladio found a type of aristocratic and ecclesiastical patronage somewhat different from other examples under consideration. He was to design a building in which the utilitarian functions were assigned a role of secondary importance. The purpose of all this was to express Almerico's ambition and cultural attainments, crowned by his sojourn in Rome. The location chosen for the villa was already known by the name "Rotonda." It was famous for its amenities and the rare beauty of the panorama, celebrated by Palladio himself: "Above a small mount of easy access, washed on one side by the Bacchiglione, a navigable river, and on the other, surrounded by other delightful hills that give it the aspect of a grand theater."

Even though the Rotonda seems a monument to itself, it still reveals a genius distinct from that of the Villa di Meledo, in that it was perfectly proportioned, yet also well rooted in the province and in the landscape, by a deeply harmonious relationship. The interior decoration, rich in stuccowork and painting, constitutes an ideal portrait, bringing together the patron's classical reminiscences and his ecclesiastical activities.

We find in this region marvelous examples of villas in which the humanistic impulse dictated, such as the *Villa Eolia*, or the "Prison of the Winds" at Costozzo, built, as Palladio writes, by the most excellent gentleman Francesco Trento.

Hot or cold air was brought to the villa from the caves and galleries of the nearby Berican Hills by a network of air ducts, rendering even more pleasant the "symposia" held there by famous personalities of the day.

The underground pavilion, which was frescoed by Giovanni Antonio Fasolo, seemed to express a new and different relationship, almost an osmosis, with the subterranean cosmos. The Eolia seemed to collect and dominate nature's most hidden and mysterious forces, suggesting an inverted parallel with Palladio's Rotonda, where the architecture fused so harmoniously with the surrounding landscape.

The Guà – which had also been variously named the Agno, the New River, the Furious, and the Frassine – was one of the rivers that finally found peace with the works carried out in the *Retratto di Lozzo*.

Just outside Lonigo, at the point where the Roman road meets the river at Bagnolo, rises the Villa dei Pisani. This Venetian family had bought at auction the properties (and hence also the ancient feudal rights) belonging to the noble Nogarola family from Verona, who had fallen into disgrace at the time of Cambrai.

Having acquired these vast holdings, the Pisani directed their energies mainly into agriculture, increasing the cultivation of rice and hemp, products that were easily shipped to the Dominante along the Guà river. It is characterized by a city

family establishing itself and bringing to the province the Venetian's practical and commercial mentality while adjusting to the customs and ambitions of the mainland's feudal, military, and chivalrous nobility.

Palladio was charged with giving this concept a form, while conferring on the villa the aura of prestige and authority that was characteristic of its builders.

In an area already known for its ancient settlements, the building conserved some of the details of

Anselmo Canera (1522–1586). Ancient sacrifice (Pojana Maggiore, Villa Pojana, Sala degli Imperatori).

the castle that preceded it. There are the two small lateral towers, while the heavy rustification of the river façade was clearly inspired by Sanmicheli.

The interior of the villa is characterized by a vast hall inspired, as Palladio said, by "the houses of the Romans." The lords of the land, representing the Serenissima, held their public functions in this hall. The villa at Bagnolo is distinguished stylistically by the presence of rather distinct elements. The monumental and robust riverfront façade stood in contrast with that which, with a classical pediment, should have opened onto the courtyard. The frescos of the vaults and walls celebrate the river for the benefits it brings in agriculture and commerce, and for the delights that it bestows on life in the villa.

Following the course of the Guà, one reaches the area of Cologna, called "of the Venetians" after May 18, 1406 when the Maggior Consiglio added it to the Dorsoduro quarter of Venice in order to end the dispute between Vicenza and Verona. There appeared in the territory of Cologna an original type of patronage linked primarily to the principalities of central Italy (the Medici, for example), rather than to Venice. All the villas of this fertile and well-cultivated land belonged to a single family, that of the Counts Serego.

It is not possible to document Palladio's activity at Veronella, at Cucca, at Miega, or Beccacivetta – all place names that appear frequently in Palladian literature. The reason for this is that only a few of these projects were ever realized.

The Villa Pisani at Montagnana is the expression of another type of commission. It stood right on a stream that, besides cooling the inhabitants, also drive the millstones of an immense mill that was first built by the Da Carrara for the needs of the territory.

Given its urban character, the villa may have been linked with this industrial activity, from which enriched the Pisani. The direct contact with marketing and distribution centers might have suggested the construction of a port facility, now impossible to envisage.

The example offered by the Villa Pojana, which lies two and a half miles (four kilometers) from Montagnana, is different and subject to analysis in two senses. One is characterized by the military component and the other by agriculture. The name of the Pojana family is related to the castle that was one of the few spared by the Venetians, perhaps as a token of gratitude for the loyalty of the family demonstrated at the time of Cambrai.

The Pojana instead were enfeoffed of the territory by the Venetians "*cum omnibus juribus et jurisdictionibus ad castellarium spectantibus.*" This commission had patently military origins, linked to the arts of war, as is evident from the austere character of the villa's architecture and the frescos that decorate it, illustrating scenes of battle, Roman emperors, and military triumphs.

Another element, however, helps to define the attitudes of the noble family. In the Hall of the Emperors a fresco represents a procession of people in Roman dress, preceded by an elder who moves toward the Temple of Peace to extinguish the torch of war on its altar, a subject obviously symbolic of the change in the times. A climate of peace spread abroad once warfare was uprooted. Even the Pojana decided to abandon military undertakings and dedicate themselves to agriculture, in the manner of the Roman soldier who left behind a trace of himself in the inscription found at Pojana: *Marcus Billienus Marci Filius/ Romana Actiacus/ Legione Xi Proelio/ Navali Facto In/ Coloniam Deductus/ Ab Ordine Decurionum Electus.* This is a particularly interesting inscription that confirms a hypothesis of mine already formulated in 1964. In studying the Veneto villas, it became apparent that they were frequently laid out to correspond with pre-existing Roman buildings. In many localities of the Basso Vicentino and particularly at Pojana, it is easy to see this link between the Roman *statio* or outpost, the medieval tower and Gothic house, and the sixteenth-century villa. The so-called *Ca Quinta* at Meledo, whose Roman origins were revealed by numerous fragments scattered in the neighborhood, provides an interesting confirmation.

Another rather complex and interesting example of patronage is offered by the villa erected by the

Saraceno at Finale di Agugliaro. It is not far from another sixteenth-century villa, the one called *delle Trombe*, attributed, not without good reason, to Michele Sanmicheli. Palladio's description of the Villa di Finale introduces the chapter in the *Four Books of Architecture* concerning the villas constructed for the mainland nobility.

The territory of Finale had been the property of the family since the fourteenth century when Pietro Saraceno, nominated Bishop of Vicenza (ecclesiastical office was always a source of wealth), moved from Rome with his entourage and his relations. Thanks to the reclamation and to the control of the waters of the Liona river, the villa rose on a site that had become rich and fertile. These factors encouraged agricultural acti-vitiy. That wealth was part of the ideals of the family is documented in a fresco in the center of one of the halls, where there is an allegorical figure of riches. The Venetian mercantile mentality had been acquired even by the mainland nobility. Notwithstanding the great achievements of his artistic production, Palladio seemed to extol a perennial Hellenism, an idealism that transforms every component through beauty. Yet in the *Four Books of Architecture* there are few references to the poetic or aesthetic qualities of the buildings described. On the contrary, it is their function-alism and utility, their practicality, and the atten-tion to the most concrete needs of everyday life that are exalted.

The Villa Emo at Fanzolo is a significant example. Only those parts associated with the working of the land and the storage of agricultural products are described. The presentation of the Villa at Finale is in the same vein, where "beneath

Andrea Palladio; The Teatro Olimpico of Vicenza.

The villas and their surroundings

It is said that Thomas Jefferson, the President of the United States, who was a great admirer and imitator of Palladio, took back cuttings of grass and plants from the Colli Berici to Monticello in Virginia, in order to recreate there surroundings similar to those of the Palladian villas. Obviously Thomas Jefferson had understood that in order to revive the art of the great architect it was first of all necessary to try to reconstruct the inseparable unity between monument and Nature.

there are the cellars and above, the granary which occupies the entire floor of the house. The kitchens are outside, but linked in such a way as is convenient. Those places necessary for the villa's functioning are found on either side."

It is natural at this point to ask which were the motives that led Palladio to this concrete realism. One should not forget that, particularly in the early period, Palladio worked primarily for particular patrons who came from the mainland nobility and saw in agriculture the sure way to accumulate in a brief time that impressive wealth that was necessary in order for these particularly ambitious minor nobles, otherwise deprived of every power in the organization of the state, to reach a position of prestige occupying public office and even acquire Venetian ennoblement.

This propensity for agriculture appears clearly documented in the presence, next to the residential block, of the *barchesse*, the outbuildings with dovecotes and services of every sort designed for the storage of farm implements and the fruits of the harvest, buildings through which Palladio kept alive the Veneto's popular culture alongside the traditions of the classics.

As is evident at Finale the granaries came to assume a fundamental importance. While the peasantry living in thatched roof huts could not conserve grain for long, the nobles could store and protect it in the villas, waiting for the periods of scarcity when they could sell it at inflated prices. The advantages accrued thus, more than justified the immense expense of erecting a great villa.

The Palladian construction at Finale reflects better than any other an agrarian reality suggesting the fusion between architecture and country. In its sobriety and its essential qualities, it constitutes a characteristic example of the villa-farm that, in order to display its utilitarian function, neglects its decorative or representational qualities.

Our research into the Palladio's presence in the Basso Vicentino concludes at *Campiglia dei Berici*. The Villa conceived there for the Repeta family was located in one of the key positions of the medieval fortification line, which touched Cologna

and Montagnana, and stretched from the territory of Verona all the way to the Euganean hills. Even in this case, the Repeta's sixteenth-century residence was none other than the expression of the need to create, even in terms of form, a sense of continuity with the arts of the past.

The Repeta had taken possession of Campiglia as early as the thirteenth century, purchasing their fief from the Bishop of Vicenza. From this moment onward, their feudal investiture would be sustained through to the fall of the Serenissima and even beyond.

Even if during the transition from the era of the city-states through that of the principalities, the system of feudal jurisdiction was reduced, the line of continuity into which the present Baroque villa, like the Palladian villa, inserted is still evident. A *domus dominicali* or nobleman's residence was built on the ruins of the castle and then replaced by the Palladian villa. After a fire destroyed this, a seventeenth-century building was built to coincide significantly in type. Important documentary evidence exists of the survival of the ancient organization, of the feudal system, and of the patronage that the lord exercised, not only over that villa or the lands subject to him, but also over the tenants and even the municipality.

The Repeta family, like the Pojana, was characterized by two fundamental attitudes, one of a military character and the other of an agricultural and cultural nature. The former aspect can be seen in the seventeenth-century reconstruction ordered by Enea Repeta, the military commander of the fortress of Verona, among other duties. Turning his back on humanistic precedents, he made for himself a closed and austere residence of a solider, flanked by an enclosure for military exercises.

Although belonging to a younger generation, Palladio considered himself the interpreter of an earlier progeny. The Villa at Campiglia, an extremely original construction among Palladio's projects was published in the *Four Books* as lacking any central elements; there was no central block flanked, as in other cases, by the *barchessas*. The villa stretched along a vast, arcaded courtyard, like an "agora." And with its open form, it led back to the model of the "Greek house" that opened out toward the country.

Palladio wrote, "This building has the convenience of being able to go everywhere under cover because that part reserved for the owners' residence and that for the farm are of the same height. That which the one loses in grandeur means that it is not more prominent than the other so the dignity and ornament of the farm building is increased, making it the equal of that of the owners for the beauty of the whole work."

The open, hospitable character of this architecture finds its counterpart in the decoration of the rooms, executed by Maganza in such a way that the room where friends were lodged would be decorated with the virtues most like them.

These egalitarian ideals stemmed from two fundamental concepts. The first, of a cultural nature, was the influence exercised by Trissino and his circle which gave a new impetus to the rediscovery of the Greeks and the study of Petrarch's poetry. The other idea resulted from the rather massive presence of the Anabaptists in this territory. This was the religious sect that preached equality, fraternity, and the withdrawal from all public office.

It remains to be seen why Palladio, in the early years of his activity, operated primarily in this particular region.

This area was among the first to profit from the reclamation work carried out by the Venetian magistrates who guaranteed noteworthy economic and commercial progress following the regulation of the waters and the intensification of agricultural activity. Vast stretches of land, formerly belonging to the religious orders, were gradually acquired by the nobility. Already in the fifteenth century they had begun to transform it into fertile land.

The climate of expectancy as well as hope that accompanied the many operations of reclamation in the region extended over several centuries, and was expressed in a letter written by Francesco Pojana where he stated his intention, "To increase his earnings as soon as the *Ritratto di Lozzo* was brought to an end."

But alone these interests of a prevalently economic character would not have led to any artistic result. It must be remembered that we find ourselves in an area strongly influenced by the lively ferment of humanism.

The amenities and the fertility of this locality contributed to the fortune of this territory as Pigafetta rightly observed: "It seems as if the spirit of an ennobled Nature designated all the excellent qualities of that sky and solid for the ease and pleasure of human life."

But one particularly interesting consideration for us concerns the very origins of Palladio's art. From many documents, we know that he began as a stonecutter in Padua in the workshop of Bartolomeo Cavazza, "stonemason." He was called "da Sossano," from his hometown, which was famous for the quarries of that soft stone that Palladio preferred for his villas.

The architect's predilection for this land where he had his first experiences as a stonecutter can be recalled in order to find a justification for the continual presence of Palladio in the Basso Vicentino. The Basso Vicentino was also where he came to know those building materials that would constitute one of the most determinant characteristics of his art.

The patrons of the villas.

In 1555 a group of "virtuous and kind spirits" from the city of Vicenza "gave life" to the Accademia Olimpica. From 1580 the erudite meetings of the Accademia were held at the Odeon and the adjacent Palladian theater, where one can see the effigies of aristocrats who had been so important in the history and culture of Vicenza. Names such as Caldogno, Trissino, and Valmarana are to be found at the feet of these statues, "dressed in the antique style," men who dominated the political events and gave their names to the prestigious country residence that still today ennoble every corner of the province. Aristocrats of refined learning, Palladio's patrons transformed their own villas into direct emanations of the Vicenza Academy.

Architectural Style until the Eighteenth Century

THE VENETO VILLAS TO THE ENDURANCE OF FEUDALISM

With the Villa of the Repeta at Campiglia one can commence a discussion on a theme that I introduced in a talk given in Vicenza in 1978 entitled "Feudalism and the Veneto Villas."

Students of history often uncover facts and laws that prove particulary useful for the interpretation of artistic phenomena. Thus, the research of historians like Gina Fasoli, Ruggero Romano, and, even more recently, Giuseppe Gullino, into the persistences of feudal custom in the Veneto can be applied to the architecture of the villa in order to illustrate a cultural turning point that should not be neglected.

The Venetian patricate, practiced in trade and governing, turned their capital from investments in commerce, which was no longer secure or remunerative. Utilizing the juridical instruments offered by custom, after having acquired landed property near waterways and possibly in zones free from duties, they provided for the economic organization of the territory, resurrecting ancient benefits or establishing new ones.

Thus Venice in 1587 found the need to institute an appropriate *Magistratura dei Provveditori sopra i Feudi*, legalizing a practice that, up to now, had existed through tradition.

In the list of the nobles who requested feudal investiture of the Magistrature, we encounter the names of many families who built some of the most celebrated villas, and who believed that feudal rights represented a title to prestige, or else simply a source of income.

The families listed by Gullino were not the only ones. In fact, there is no record of the Repeta, who obtained an investiture at Campiglia, as appeared in a document of 1703 concerning the properties of the Villa Repeta at Campiglia dei Berici.

This confirmation of an investiture was granted to Enea and Scipione, brothers of the Manfredi-Repeta family, "nobles of our city of Vicenza."

As is apparent in the same document, the investiture involved a "fraternity" or family partnership by Venetian disposition. It established the indivisibility of the patrimony "to the end that such a noble capital and patrimony be conserved undivided."

Among other things, it may be observed that the names of the two brothers were Roman names. That they constructed a palace out of the ancient relic of the castle of Campiglia represented a continuity with the past. The inscription on the façade of the villa of Campiglia represented other evidence of this remaking of the past: "Remade by us in a nobler form."

We have already mentioned the military tradition of the Repeta family. Before becoming nobles, they were qualified in the document as "extremely loyal Sargents-General in Battle." The cult of military traditions also appeared on the vaster horizon of the cult of Antiquity. The same Palladio, such a profound cultivator of the antique, revealed his interest in martial arts. He spoke of military exercises in the book and the way in which they followed a ritual, taken from the writings of Caesar and how, in the end, the art of war ought to be considered the most excellent among the arts.

Another important aspect was the continuity of investiture that should pass to the masculine descendents of the Repeta "ad infinitum," an indication that everything was done to last throughout time. Building was done not for today but for eternity. This document of 1703 probably had precedents that went back to the fifteenth century when the Repeta entered into Venetian service. It is also likely that it had been confirmed during the days of Cambrai. Perhaps this feudalization was exclusively a phenomenon of the sixteenth and seventeenth centuries, but there are good reasons for believing that it goes back further in time.

Through this investiture Venice recognized the feudal rights of the Repeta, admitting the feoff even though not conferring the civil and criminal jurisdiction recognized for the Feudatories of Meledo and Alonte.

In 1820, the Austrian Government confirmed the ancient nobility of the Repeta. In 1854 the Imperial and Royal Fiscal Office obtained the devolution to the state of the feudal possessions of Campiglia after the death of the last legitimate heir. In 1868, following a trial for the illegal ownership of the fief of Campiglia, Alvise Mocenigo obtained, with the payment of the sum of 95,000 lire – according to a law of the Kingdom of Italy, dated January 24, 1864 – the right to state that his possessions at Campiglia and at Sossano remained "free and immune from any feudal bond or any feudal tax."

The feudal tradition was deeply rooted and should be kept in mind in the study of the *World of the Veneto Villas*. Notwithstanding its negative aspects, this feudalism, even if of a particular type in terms of its relationship with the republican state of Venice, did determine the character and the fortune of entire area of the Veneto.

THE VILLA IN THE SEVENTEENTH CENTURY

The seventeenth century in the Veneto was distinguished by the assertion of a new patricate, who assumed the duty of keeping the ancient republic alive in the face of a new vision of the world that was becoming more evident in Europe. Thus the ideals of the republic were constantly being adjusted to the mentality of an ambitious and assertive obligarchy. At the beginning of the century, Paolo Sarpi and his congregation of political friends had vainly attempted to furnish the state with new and more adequate structures. He even tried to bring the Porto Viro canal to completion, an enormous undertaking that prevented the Po river's outlets from silting up the lagoon.

The deep disturbances of the period can be seen in the abandonment of the principal way that, notwithstanding the Venetians' multiform experiences, had given a kind of unity to their arts and thought. Andrea Palladio remained the great master in architecture. There were moments of extravagance with the introduction to the Veneto lands of those grandiose architectonic structures that enjoyed such great success with the courts of central Europe. Despite the lack of really brilliant architects, the better part of the Veneto villas assumed their actual appearance precisely in this

century. The causes for this were numerous. In general it can be stated that in the course of the seventeenth century, a propitious historical moment was coming to maturity which corresponded to this art. For example, after the terrible plague of 1630 the great number of victims made for an even greater concentration of landed property in the hands of a few landholding magnates. In addition, between 1645 and 1649 the War of Candia reduced the reserves of the Venetian state,

Pietro Longhi: The Feudatary (Venice, Pinacoteca Querini Stampalia). No written text can explain better the subject of this painting, the relationship between the authority of the master and the respectfulness of the peasants.

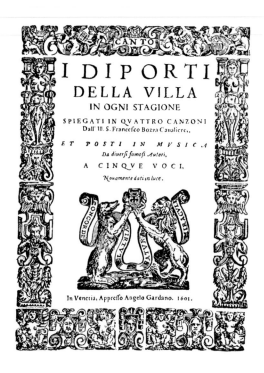

Palladian works that were left incomplete because of the financial crisis and the plague were taken up again and brought to completion. If so many buildings were requested from the Vicentine master's followers or from the foremen who had faithfully worked by his side, this was due to the existence of this new, ambitious patricate. Thus, for example, that which Palladio had merely suggested in the incompleted project for the Villa Tissino at Meledo, was now completely carried out.

The restoration and restructuring of ancient agrarian residences was very frequent, although these were often little more than the rustic huts that had populated the countryside in the course of the sixteenth century. Consolidated economic power, secure earnings guaranteed by landed investment, rising ambitions, and the anxiety to display visibly one's own proper political function, pushed these patricians to a detailed ennobling of rural villas, whose rather rough and simple architecture was now covered over in sculpture and decorative elements. A new sort of management, which might be defined as feudal, appeared in this context in the country and justified itself. This has been illustrated in the case of Campiglia. Later on we shall examine other similar evidence.

This was the period in which the Manin, having acquired an incalculable number of properties, made themselves into a feudal power on which Venice could depend to control the entire region.

It can also be found at Piazzola on the Brenta in the Villa Contarini-Camerini, one of the largest buildings in the Veneto country, enlarged and covered with baroque decoration around the mid-century. Preceded by a semicircular portico enclosing a vast area fitted out as a market – today the principal village square – the villa offered its guests every sort of amusement: fish ponds, race tracks, parks, gardens, and concert halls, all according to the taste and fashion of the times.

In many cases the village organized itself in urbanistic terms as a function of these villas. The economic development of Noventa Vicentina received a stimulus from the agricultural activity that the Barbarigo promoted in the area.

which was obliged from 1646 onward to sell a large number of public holdings that had been expropriated – in the period of the requisitions – from the Della Scala and the Da Carrara.

The proceeds were not sufficient to meet the needs of the war and, on payment of enormous sums of money, they were obliged to welcome to the ranks of the Venetian nobility, seventy-seven mainland families, and then in 1684, during the War in the Peloponese, another forty-seven families were similarly admitted to noble rank.

The ambitions and economic possibilities of these new patricians found adequate interpretation in architecture and in all the artistic expression of the Venetian seventeenth century.

Palladio's architecture, which had spread abroad and was by now imitated even outside the Veneto and Italy, seemed the best suited to illustrate the glories of these new patricians just as it had done for the most famous families of the Veneto provinces in the second half of the sixteenth century.

Their villa at Noventa, built at the end of the sixteenth century, determined in the end even the position of the parish church. Abandoning the traditional east-west orientation, it was rebuilt parallel to the Barbarigo's palace in the middle of the seventeenth century. A clearly seventeenth-century mentality seems to have guided both the execution of the frescos that celebrate the glories and triumphs of the family, as well as the rearrangement of the gardens, personally carried out by Senator Giovanni Barbarigo.

Despite the flowering of grandiose, theatrical villas, one can say that the seventeenth century in the Veneto was substantially poor in true architects capable of brilliant solutions. Frequently, we find ourselves in front of pretentious, inorganic buildings, of added-on architecture that overwhelms the previous structures, or else bizzare and hardly functional solutions characterized by the lack of a unifying spirit. In general one notes a change in the typology, despite the fact that the lessons of Palladio persisted in some area. Often the broad colonnades and the classicizing pediments were abandoned in favor of less well-articulated architecture, of the heavy unsymmetrical palaces that are illustrated in Coronelli's and Volkamer's famous engravings.

The Veneto villas of the seventeenth century repeat previous types more or less, often weighing them down and adding more movement to both decorations and structures. The central hall was given maximum importance, evident from the outside because of the raised elevation crowned with a pediment or dome. This hall, two stories tall, would be interupted halfway up by a hanging gallery into which the doors and windows of the upper rooms opened. The most famous painters of the period were often called to decorate the walls and ceilings of these villas. Walls were transformed into fantastic mythological and historical scenes, which anticipated the gradiosity of Tiepolo's decoration.

The taste for the spectacular predominated. Both pictorial and sculptural decoration received a great impulse, to the extent that patrons were obliged to turn to foreign artists. There was also

an increase in the love of gardens, which now replaced the villa's adjacent fields. Everywhere was found the desire to astonish, to dazzle with water works, bizzare sculptural groups, fountains, fish ponds, towers, and labyrinths.

In the Rocco Pisana, Scamozzi seemed to crown the Palladian ideal of a perfect fusion between the villa and the surrounding landscape. He did not limit himself to planning the patrician residence, but personally undertook to modify the shape of the hill, making it assume the appearance of a great snail's shell crowned by the purest architecture that

An engraving of a water-show on one of the fish ponds of villa Contarini at Piazzola sul Brenta (L'orologio del Piacere, Piazzola, 1685).

59

Paolo Veronese, Diana, a detail from the fresco on the ceiling of the Sala dell'Olimpo (Maser, Villa Barbaro).

Scamozzi: the scientific, the attention to the natural environment, international culture, the taste for the theatrical (recalling the Theatre at Sabbioneta or his contributions to the Olimpico), and the curiosity for European novelties.

The art of Scamozzi has a place of great importance that surpasses even the limits of his time. Inspired in his severe rationalism by the architects of the sixteenth century, he contributed to limiting the spread of the bizzare and jagged shapes of Baroque taste in the Veneto provinces, constituting moreover a valid premise for the re-emergence of neoclassical tendencies in the eighteenth century.

The reawakening of the love for the country coincided, in the eighteenth century, with a repetition of Palladian models carried out by a range of Veneto architects.

THE FRESCOS OF THE VENETO VILLAS

The admiration which the villas of the Veneto have always inspired is due to an architectonic typology, to the materials of which they are constructed, to the accurate choice of the setting (such as Palladio himself always used for each complex conceived by him), and to the beauty of the gardens and parks. But their form was also linked to their peculiar function in the Venetian dominion, to the historical significance assumed in the organization of the mainland and differently experienced according to the cultural epoch. Although modes of life and models of architecture can change, the gentleman's sojourn in the country was always experienced or dreamed of as taking place in a place of delight, alleviated by landscape visions, inspired by spaces opening onto a dominant nature.

Although architecture expressed the ideas and the practical needs that have given birth to the villa, the discussion becomes more explicit if we stop to consider the painting and the plastic decoration that ornamented the interiors. This represented a language, which, from the sixteenth century, would contribute to making the source of the villa, its culture, and the fantasies of its inhabitants even more explicit.

completely reveals the ideals of the artist. He put the "dignity" or worthiness, clearly visible in a "high place," in the first place of his hierarchy of values. "The high place in comparison with the lower is like a comparison between form and material. As is known the form precedes the other in dignity." Scamozzi's poetics also seemed to have been in full accord with the new orientation of the Pisani, who sought pure air and aristocratic isolation in these hills, far from the cares of town life (in the center of Lonigo, they owned a great town palace) and from the duties connected with the management of the immense properties at Bagnolo. The spirit of the architect – outlined in his classification of the various types of villa – seems to find a complete realization in this building, whose relationships with its surroundings is substantially based on the hedonistic complacency of admiring a nature organized by man. This same Scamozzi revealed himself to be an excellent town planner (a quality, as Milizia says, he inherited from his father) not only in his ability to harmonize his buildings with the landscape but also in his restructuring of an entire urban center, as he did in Salzburg. One can say that all of the principal tendencies of the century are summarized in

It is enough to recall the names of some artists in order to understand the importance of this chapter in history: Paolo Veronese at Maser; Alessandro Vittoria at Montagnana; Zeolotti at Fanzolo; Giallo Fiorentino at Fratta Polesine; Sustris at Luvigliano; Marinali at Trissino; Dorigny at Grezzana; Zais at Stra; the Tiepolo at Vicenza and at Zianigo; Demin at Conegliano.

Normally Venetian houses were decorated on their exteriors. According to Michelangelo the entire city appeared as a "beautiful painting." Transplanting painting to the interior meant creating it for the sole pleasure of the inhabitants and their guests. Thus it was, for example, for the Ca d'Oro, painted with scenes of hunting and gardens. Little by little, as the ideal of modern man acquired a clearer aspect, there was evidence, along with developments in architecture, of the internal decoration of the villas.

One of the first and most interesting examples of fresco in a villa was that desired by Alvise Cornaro to decorate the niches of the Odeon in the music room; landscapes and views were designed with a certain illusionism as if they were windows through which one regarded the country. This motif would find masterly expression in the sixteenth century, for example, in Veronese's frescos at the Villa Barbaro at Maser. False arches introduced the spectator to realistic country landscapes where ruins of antique Rome perpetuated the dream of an ideal continuity between modern patrons and the ancients associated with those magnificent buildings.

The frescos underlined or narrated, more or less clearly, the functions fulfilled by the villa. The conception of the villa was always in perfect harmony with its dimensions and importance (for example there were no representations of Olympus in rooms not sufficiently spacious).

Studies and theories that concern "grotesques" – always considered representative of a universal language of pagan iconology – always end by involving artists of the Veneto. The grotesque genre, happily exemplified at the Villa Badoer at Fratta Polesine and executed by Giallo Fiorentino, often recurred in the decoration of villa interiors.

Giambattista Tiepolo. A detail from the Clemency of Scipio (Montecchio Maggiore, Villa Cordellina).

In the Villa dei Vescovi at Luvigliano, Sustris inserted figures alluding to the prestige of the Duke among the landscapes and the grotesques; at Maser Veronese portrayed his patrons, capturing them in the most homely attitudes, next to decorative jokes designed to amuse and puzzle the spectator – the little girl opening a door to spy on the guest, the dog asleep, the broom left behind, etc.

In eighteenth-century frescos the most often recurring themes were taken from poetry. Scenes of the *Pastor Fido* were painted by Carpioni in the Villa Caldogno and also by Celesti in the Villa Rinaldi at Caesell d'Asolo. Or again, historical themes like the foundation of Padua were taken from a literary source at the Villa Selvatico at Battaglia Terme. With the function of the villa no longer exclusively agricultural, the hunt became a common subject, as at the Villa Contarini at Piazzola. The concept of amusement and hospitality on holiday became a primary motif in the eighteenth century as the proprietor's personal interest in the cultivation of the land diminished. The need to renew the villa rooms in terms of this new concept of holiday use became the occasion for the displays of the proprietor's wealth and generosity, with a renewed profusion of interior decoration now quite independent of the external architecture.

Historical subjects appeared in fresco where the theme of the banquet predominated, as at the Villa Marcello at Levada and in the Villa Giovanelli at Noventa. These were often placed in settings influenced by Algarotti's neo-Palladianism.

The taste for simulation in both landscape and architectural subjects was still alive at the Villa Garzadori, where the paintings with ruins were designed to suit the "Grotto" built into the complex. These frescos, which had lost the sixteenth century's moralizing key, now bespoke pleasure and Arcadian leisure: games and hunts at the Villa Albrizzi at Preganziol; fantasies and architectural views in the Villa Mocenigo at Canda; astrology with the signs of the Zodiac, or battles between Centaurs and Giants as recounted by Dorigny in the Villa Arvedi at Grezzana.

Views of distant places were introduced to reflect the nobleman's love of travel. Rigid in their conservatism the nobles assigned the representation of their cultural environment to Giambattista Tiepolo. Thus, we can see in the Villa Cordellina how this artist with theatrical sensitivity bestowed praise on the patron with the historical subject of Alexander and Scipio, alluding to the virtues of magnanimity and clemency. Episodes taken from literature in the Villa Valmarana ai Nani (the *Gerusalemme Liberata*, *Orlando Furioso*, and the *Aeneid*) probably served to mask, with epic and chivalrous costumes, the spiritual uncertainty that characterized the aristocratic class in that era.

Even the bourgeoisie in this period took up the "villa holiday craze" of going to the country , which was immortalized in the pages of Goldoni. Giandomenico Tiepolo, one of the finest decorators interpreting the bourgeois taste, increasingly moved away from the assurance and the easy triumphalism of his father.

At the same time, the echo of the Orient is increasingly heard. The chinoiserie that Giandomenico attempted in the Villa Valmarana went with Rococo taste, contributing, along with the stuccowork, to the break up of the decoration of the rooms, once frescoed with mythologies and histories. In the nineteenth century this taste for orientalizing and exotic motifs, such as that at the Villa Foscarini at Stra, continued to spread.

The conception of the villa as a place of escape was maintained in this century, yet, on the other hand, a distinctly utilitarian frame of mind could also reduce the villa to a simple place of agriculture or craft.

In the context of the proprietor's budgets, the demolition of "passive" parts of the villa complex was frequent. The new bourgeoisie, enriched by industry (textile and mining), preferred to display their prestige by building a new building worthy of the "status" they had achieved. They called in artists that continued the tradition of interesting fresco work.

At the Villa Revedin Bolasco at Castelfranco, built after the demolition of the preceding structure in the style of Scamozzi, Giacomo Casa presented the theme of festivities and masked balls with originality. The protagonists were dressed in eighteenth-century costumes, reviving the carefree atmosphere and the happiness of a particular page in the history of the Veneto.

Elsewhere historical themes were taken up according to a precise programme that guided painting around the mid-century. Thus frescos in the Villa Gera at Conegliano Giovanni Demin, treated episodes of Roman history, with particular attention to the encounters between the Romans and the Helvetians.

Even illusionist painting found a way to flourish again with particularly pleasing effects, as at the Villa Revedin Bolasco, where false loggias frame the scene. Thus a centuries' long tale of painting in the Veneto that reached its maximum splendor in the sixteenth century, was concluded with a sort of dignified inventory of the various genres of decoration.

THE GARDENS OF THE VENETO VILLAS

Whoever visits the Veneto villas today can imagine the splendor of the world of these villas only with difficulty because, even where their architecture remains more or less intact, their gardens, the true stars of the villa holiday, have almost all disappeared. Only by leafing through old documents one can gain an idea of the increasing importance that they assumed, so much so that the villa could be reduced to a scenic backdrop destined to be seen as a background to the garden.

The plan that evolved with the Veneto gardens remained constant until the eighteenth century when, alongside the central axis of stairs or of avenue, more importance was given to the natural element and optical effects of perspective, of arches, columns, porticoes, steps, and gates, that sought a more harmonious relationship with a vast and free natural landscape.

Topiary art, the art of the garden, was remade from an ancient tradition. The examples of the Roman classical world were alive in the organization and in the symbolic function of the garden, as well as in the villa house. The classical world proposed a structure borrowed from the model of the "paradise" of Persia (the Orient always inspired admiration and the desire to emulate), where a network of canals, the central presence of a small lake, the distribution of the fruit trees and flowers, with space for hunting and fishing, made the garden into a kind of image of the universe.

The idea of the *hortus conclusus* was taken from the theories of Martial and developed in medieval literary sources, as well as being realized concretely in monastic cloisters and gardens. Inside a green precinct, the grape vine near a fountain alluded to another life, which in Eden found its proper expression in the happy chromatic distribution of flowers and plants. In Boccaccio's *Decameron* the country could be a refuge from the mishaps of the town: the ideal place for the flowering of idylls and for refined conversations. The humanist's garden inserts itself in the nostalgic dream of Roman villas, and in the polemic between the city and the country already present in Petrarch's proposals for a "solitary life." Petrarch had, in fact, selected the place most adapted to repose, far from the anxieties of the city, amid the Euganean hills. He spent his time in more precious activity in the shadow of his vineyard, alternating his studies with poetic creativity.

Poets and writers anticipated the taste for landscape that, among painters, developed in the fifteenth century. It is sufficient to recall Stefano da Verona, Carpaccio, Giambellino, Cima da Conegliano, for whom the love of roses, gardens,

Stefano da Verona; A detail from "The Madonna of the Rose-garden" (Verona, Museo di Castelvecchio).

Orazio Marinali, Pantalone, one of the statues which populate the garden of Villa Conti Lampertico known as "La Deliziosa", at Montegaldella.

and orchards appear in such a dominant fashion as if such natural elements had an immense importance in everyday life. Trees of golden apples, scented grasses, flowered meadows, the clear waters of streams in an atmosphere of crystalline air, amid music and perfume, appear in miniatures, in tapestries, in paintings, as in the treatises and poems. Enchanting scenery reveals itself in a season of eternal spring, as if attempting to recapture the pagan "Golden Age" or the Christian's "Earthly Paradise" as in the fresco of the months in the Torre Aquila in Trento. These examples of gardens, which have disappeared, preserve the characteristics of the "enclosed garden" that still flourishes: high walls, lawns, entwined hedges, rose gardens, bushes, fruit trees like the pomegranate and orange trees, evergreen woods, beds of flowers, herbs and vine pergolas, fountains, and canals for the fish ponds or for irrigation.

After the last fortifications had disappeared from the mainland under the republic's pressing policy of expansion and economic renewal, the Venetian aspiration to greenery constrained between water and marble could finally extend itself beyond the closed gardens of Murano, the gardens of the Giudecca and those "visions of flowers" restricted to terraces and city palaces.

Palladio in particular felt the link between the habitation and its natural environment, whether it was a vast landscape or a setting created by man in such a way that all the elements were recomposed in a single harmony. "Having found the site, happy, pleasant, comfortable, and healthy," he said, "the elegant and commodious rearrangement is required" in such a way that "the gentleman will derive great utility and consolation from the villa where he will pass his time in taking care of and ornamenting his possessions, increasing them with his labors and the arts of agriculture. His body will conserve its health and strength easily, taking that exercise on foot and on horseback that the villa affords and where, finally, the soul, tired of the agitations of the city, will be restored and will find consolation."

Water, as in antiquity, assumed a particular value. While the fish ponds had a function that was not only functional but also utilitarian, and the canals and streams created a musical atmosphere, the fountains, placed in the key points of the perspectives, served to emphasize the forms and proportions of the gardens. Inasmuch as it was the "*fons salutis*" as in ancient cloisters, the fountain's symbolic value was often repeated in the statues that surmounted it. In the same way, the figures completed an allegorical program in the nymphei which often bordered the secret gardens, as at Maser.

Only in the second half of the sixteenth century, did the garden, even though remaining fundamentally within the Veneto tradition, tend to a kind of exhibitionism that demonstrated the nobility and wealth of the landlord in an atmosphere of feudal restoration.

Between the seventeenth and eighteenth century gardens became increasingly rich in surprises, labyrinths, open air theaters, follies. They were populated with statues that evoked a mythologicalor literary culture, as in the park of the Villa Rinaldi at Casella d'Asolo.

The art of the garden spread everywhere in the Veneto, but perhaps there was a particular expansion in the area around Treviso and along the Brenta, where the Venetian city dwellers chose to establish their country residences. Because of the great fashion for holidays in the villas, the gardens were no longer only the goal of the solitary meditative spirit, but now welcomed and delighted the carefree holiday makers and their guests.

Parks were constructed with thick shadows through which woodland gods could be glimpsed, and where the noise of some fountain or specially constructed cascade could be heard. Strolls in the park were guided by avenues that intersected according to the principal axes and by the paths that led off them, bringing the visitor to the mysteries of the labyrinth, to the surprises of aquatic jokes, and the secrets of the nymphaeum. But we find another memory of humanistic culture in the pride with which rare and precious plants were exhibited. One of the most peculiar elements of the villas in Volkamer's engraved decoration seems to be the greenhouses because of the enthusiasm with which they were planted and the rare varieties that they contained.

Thus, the new taste of the eighteenth century emerged in juxtaposition to the geometric schemes of the Renaissance, suggesting the capricious and the unforeseen, with bizarre inventive effects of perspective, of waters, springs, and labyrinths according to the theatrical vocation of a society that, the more it approached its end, the more it exalted noble "appearances."

But by the end of the eighteenth century, there appeared a reaction against a rationally organized nature. This was a romantic "naturalism" that had developed primarily in England.

In the "English garden," – which spread quickly in Italy and whose culture was promulgated even by certain Veneto artists and academicians – the ideal returned to a picturesque disorder in nature translated in the construction of tiny lakes, artificial hills, classical or neo-Gothic temples, tortuous paths, false ruins, oriental-style elements (like pagodas), and even the introduction of tropical and exotic plants that gave an unusual note to the nineteenth-century garden. All this suggested the idea of a free environment in which the most diverse plants grow spontaneously, while willow trees, which enjoyed an enormous popularity, suggested a noble melancholy.

Ludovico Pozzoserrato; a concert in the garden (Treviso, Museo Civico).

Lifestyle and Architecture of Villas in the Eighteenth and Nineteenth Centuries

The Veneto Villas of the Eighteenth Century in the Pages of Carlo Goldoni

The Veneto villas had an exceptional chronicler in the eighteenth century. It was Carlo Goldoni who was always an attentive observor of the "World," his declared "Master."

There is no lack of comedies set in the country in Goldoni's work. Some took place in the ancient "feudal" properties and one, written in 1752, is even called *Il Feudatario* or the feudatory.

It is the day of taking possession of the fief, and the community of Montefosco is getting ready to take "the oath of vassalage." But the new lord, a profligate young Marquess, in memory of ancient rights, seeks to "enfeoff" the peasants' women.

However, times have changed. The "deputies and syndics" of the "ancient and noble community" have decided to "defend the possession of

Portrait of Carlo Goldoni, an engraving by Giambattista Pitteri from a painting by Piazetta (Venice, Museo Correr).

their honor and their reputation" and in the third act of this comedy, thanks to a solemn beating, the Marquess will be forced to gentler attitudes.

But the great feudatories interested Goldoni relatively little. He was the representative of a bourgeoisie, the new managerial class, holding out against the structure of a world headed for its eclipse. Goldoni did not tire of telling the bourgeoisie, especially in the comedy of 1761 called *Le Smanie per la Villegiatura* (or The Craze for Villa Holidays), not to exceed the limits of their condition, not to ruin themselves by competing with "the Florentine Marquisses who have fiefs and enormous holdings and offices and grandiose dignity."

He spoke of Florence as elsewhere he spoke of Livorno or Napoli, but in reality he was always dealing with Venice. The model of the older generation was compared to the new generation that let itself be taken in by the "craze for villa holidays," because of the "ambition of the little who wish to impress the great" (as one reads in the preface to that comedy). They knew how to administer the earnings of the country and thus established the period of their visits to the villas in the season of the harvest. "In my times, when I was young," says a character in the same comedy, "One went early to the villa and returned early to the city. Once the wine was made, one returned to the city. But then one went in order to make the wine. Today one goes for amusement and one stays in the country with the cold, watching the leaves dry up on the trees."

"These holidays, which were introduced for the pleasure and profit of the citizenry," writes Goldoni in the introduction to his comedy of 1755 entitled *I Malcontenti*, "Have today reached an excess of luxury of expense and of uncomfortable bondage." Even the amusement of a virtuous Arcadia, the natural companion of ancient "good government," is now displaced by the superficial splendors of continual festivity. "I remember my father, who brought with him to the country, learned doctors, men of letters, and musicians... Alas, that's not the fashion now. One wants happy people, happy people. Dance, sing, play jokes, spend happily, spend happily," says a lady, and she

is echoed by Roccolino, a "professional" holiday-maker with his fashionable French, "*Allegraman toujour, allegraman toujour*."

Like the "sponger" Ferdinando in the second act of the *Smanie*, "He was used to going to the country, not for amusement, but as a job."

In the last decades of the eighteenth century the cycle of the seasons and the hours of the day were ignored. A character in a comedy of 1755 titled *La Villeggiatura* declares, "One goes on holiday when the autumn is already finished and one turns night into day with gambling, gossip, and amorous intrigue." "There [in Venice] terrific decorum, and here liberty: one plays, one strolls, one gossips, and if every once in a while one gets into a jam, here no one says anything. The country seems to permit what the city forbids," says a character in *La Castalda* of 1751.

In this way customs were corrupted and as the bourgeoisie aped the great nobles, the inhabitants of the country were no longer content with their humble life. "The holiday-makers bring with them," one reads in the preface to the *Smanie*, "The pomp and tumult of the cities, poisoning the pleasures of the peasants and the shepherds who take their misery from their landlord's pride."

Recalling phrases from the first two acts and from the preface of the *Smanie*: "Today the country is under greater subjection to the city"; women make for the occasion "an arsenal of things"; the table silver is never sufficient because "in the country one must keep open house" and "troops of friends" come and "there will be gambling, a great feast of dancing." Whoever does not flaunt himself in the country is socially disqualified. "A year without a holiday in the villa! What will they say of me at Montenero? What will they say of me in Livorno? I won't be able to look anyone in the face again." "If she does not go to the country, she will die before the month is out."

No great prophet was needed to guess that "the grandiosity of the villa" would lead to "misery in the city" for the "little ones" who for "ambition" hope to "make an impression with the great." The products of the country, which were already the city dweller's major source of income, were no longer sufficient to pay for the luxury of these villa holidays. Here is the significant dialogue between Vittoria and the servant Paolo in the second act of the same comedy:

Vittoria: In the country there will be wheat.

Paolo: There won't even be enough to make the bread we need.

Vittoria: The grapes won't have been sold.

Paolo: Even the grapes are sold.

Vittoria: Even the grapes?

It is no wonder that behind this urban bourgeoisie, which does not even take the trouble to look after its own interests, a new category came to the fore that aspired to become bourgeois and

Francesco Guardi; Villa in the Trevigiano (London, formerly in the Rothermeere Collection).

supplant the landlords. These were the managers and factors who, living in the country and knowing their work, enriched themselves behind the backs of the old landowners, accumulating enough money to acquire the land on which they had been working. "Poor landowners! These foremen and factors," one reads in the first act of *Castalda* (1751) "they are assassinating us."

The fact that the old landowning class was conscious of its ruin did not attenuate, but rather aggravated the situation. It revealed their moral incapacity to act. Thus Momolo complains in the comedy of 1739 called *Il Prodigo*, which was earlier called *Momolo on the Brenta:* "Certainly no one thinks much of me. They all know the factor. That's because I let him take too many liberties. One day he'll be my landlord. I don't know what to say. I'm so spoiled that it's all right with me to amuse myself without thinking about anything."

Even the servants were aware of how things were going. They recognized their boss in whoever issued orders and had the money to back them: "Where have you taken the grain?" Momolo asks Truffaldino in the third act of the *Prodigo*, and

Truffaldino answers, "I took the grain from this house and brought it to the boss's granary."

"The boss? and who's this boss?"

Truffaldino: "The factor."

Momolo: "The factor's the boss, you ass?"

Truffaldino: "I am not an ass, sir."

Even a lowly creature like Truffaldino knew how to defend his dignity before a degraded superior.

The *Castalda*, like the *Prodigo*, took place on the Brenta: "The scene takes place in the villa of Pantalone on the Brenta, the famous resort of the Venetians."

Certainly the fame of these holidays derived from the magnificent villas and the splendid life of the great nobles. But alongside the princely residences there were an increasing number of modest villas of the Venetian bourgeoisie represented by the character of Pantaleone, who invested his earnings from commerce in landed property.

It was natural that the Venetian bourgeoisie took their manners and their scale of living with them to the villas. In the eighteenth century, these country houses often reproduced the Venetian house with its central hall and lateral living rooms.

They would be given a little character by a modest pediment on the façade, two small statues on the gate posts, recalling, on a bourgeois scale, the dignity of the ancient noble villa.

THE VILLA OF THE TIEPOLO FAMILY AT ZIANIGO

In 1759, Giambattista Tiepolo received a conspicuous compensation from the patriarch Daniele Dolfin for the frescos in a church at Udine. With these new riches Tiepolo could, according to the fashion of the day, construct a villa on their land at Zianigo. This house was probably never used by Giambattista, who was constantly away on jobs. The frescos of the villa (now at Ca' Rezzonico) were executed by his son Giandomenico in a period between 1759 to 1797. Little by little, significantly different themes and styles succeeded one another according to the changing personal and psychological circumstances of an artist who was gradually freeing himself from his father's teaching.

As in Goya's house, one can understand otherwise undocumented aspects of Giandomenico through his painting in the Villa at Zianigo. In fact, it was here that he could give free rein to his personal way of seeing, freed from the restrictions of a commission.

In order not to conflict with the dictates of official painting, Giambattista as well as Giandomenico relegated the more unconventional subjects to the guest wing of the Villa Valmarana ai Nani near Vicenza.

Free from agreements or compromises, Giandomenico took up at Zianigo the theme of the *New World* already introduced at Vicenza, here treating it with greater dramatic effect.

The ceiling of the *portego* or main gallery hall (the most important room on the ground floor) was among the earliest frescos of the Villa at Zianigo. It represented the *Triumph of Painting* over the other arts, which, executed in 1759, was still heavily indebted to his father's model. Still in '59 we see Giandomenico engaged in the chapel on the ground floor. In a series of frescos he depicted episodes from the life of San Gerolamo Miani, founder of the Somascho Order to which his brother Giuseppe belonged.

In 1764 the Tiepolos left for Madrid, aware of being artists worthy of celebrating the glories of a court. Saddened by the imminent departure, Giandomenico represented a Rinaldo that two friends and companions in arms drag away from Armida. Rinaldo directs his thoughts rather than his glance to her. She is recognizable in the statue that dominates the garden scene. His melancholy is so realistically treated that he seems to personify the artist himself, obliged to leave those beloved places to follow his father's dreams of glory.

This unique literary reference at Zianigo is evidence of a relationship with the same themes taken from the literature of chivalry at the Valmarana in 1757.

After his father's death and disillusionment with Spain, where Mengs was preferred, and having requested and been refused readmission to the Academy of Venice, Giandomenico returned in 1771 to his country house, which had remained in his brother Giuseppe's hands.

He set to frescoing the dining room with satyrs and centaurs. There seemed to be a return to the mythical "Golden Age," and to the secret life of the ancients, as a complete break with his father's heroic and divine decorative programs.

From this moment Giadomenico Tiepolo worked assiduously in his villa, far from the paternal rhetoric that patrons still required of him. Here he could finally express his vision of the world and his artistic personality, no longer bound by the models of mythology and legend. He turned to the world around him with a subtle criticism of society, often sprinkled with sarcasm.

The scene of the *Minuet* and the *Promenade* seems to document that evasive spirit, fatuous and lacking in moral fiber, that animated eighteenth-century society in the Veneto.

One can distinguish an even more disquieting aspect in the *Promenade*. Characters that head toward a distant goal and who recall the "citizens" of the Revolution are depicted in the background.

These characters could represent a society that heads toward new forms bringing with them new hopes. The most significant scene, and undoubtedly the most ironic, is to be found in the fresco of the "New World." The charlatan shows the motley crowd (perhaps because the different classes can find moments of contact only in the world of illusion) fascinating visions from a magic lantern, which attract the curiosity of the onlookers seeking ideas, or rather new truths. Both the vulgar peasant, as well as the aristocrat, are attracted to the booth and its evasion of reality and duty. They crowd together, deprived of an identity, emblems of a decadent society that has forgotten the character of its own appearance. On the left, a Pulcinella stands aloof observing these people who appear to be the new marionettes.

This fresco is not usual in the art of the Veneto in the eighteenth century. We do not find in it any of the graces of Arcadia or the caprices of the Rococo, nor the heroic and disciplined themes seen in neoclassicism.

The art of Giandomenico cannot be considered only as an adaptation of his father's art, even if he did conserve, while bringing it to maturity, the character of the language of the vignette.

A last phase in the pictorial cycle at Zianigo is dated 1797, which coincided with the moment of the fall of the republic. All the enthusiasm and the illusions referred to by a group of enlightened conservatives are put away. These frescos represent the "Adventures of Pulcinella." The world that is presented to us is the world of imaginary characters that laugh at every aspect of social life. The Pulcinellas, who are deprived of any identity by their masks, symbolize a society which was plunged into ruin because of the aristocracy's incapacity and indifference, where it is possible to survive only through an unconscious evasion.

Giandomenico Tiepolo;
Pulcinella in love.

Giandomenico Tiepolo;
The Acrobats.

II. The Villas

Petrarch's House
Arquà Petrarca, Padua

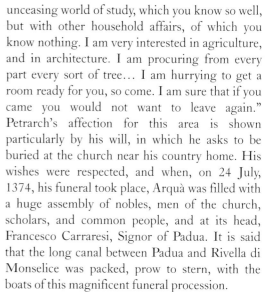

In about the year 1360, Francesco Petrarca, a guest of the Carraresi, Signori of Padua, was able to have a small house, modest but seemly, built for himself at Arquà, near the spring where the villagers went to draw their water. Here, far from his birthplace and the cares of the world, the poet was able to realize his dream of leading a serene existence, absorbed in his studies, among the gentle Euganean hills in intimate contact with nature. He had chosen the small village of Arquà in order to escape the noise and dust of the city, and to dedicate himself to study, to poetry, and other fine diversions. "The countryside is always lovely, always full of attractions to those who have noble dispositions," he wrote to a friend, "and so I am not only occupied with the ancient and unceasing world of study, which you know so well, but with other household affairs, of which you know nothing. I am very interested in agriculture, and in architecture. I am procuring from every part every sort of tree... I am hurrying to get a room ready for you, so come. I am sure that if you came you would not want to leave again." Petrarch's affection for this area is shown particularly by his will, in which he asks to be buried at the church near his country home. His wishes were respected, and when, on 24 July, 1374, his funeral took place, Arquà was filled with a huge assembly of nobles, men of the church, scholars, and common people, and at its head, Francesco Carraresi, Signor of Padua. It is said that the long canal between Padua and Rivella di Monselice was packed, prow to stern, with the boats of this magnificent funeral procession.

Although the life-style that Petrarch was extolling was completely new and original at the time, it was really a reproposal of the ideals of the ancient, classic world. We only have to remember, as Ackerman does, that alongside the villas of the powerful were those of the men of letters, such as the "Sabine fields" praised by Horace, which "were hidden in the mountains in a spectacular location which seemed to have been created especially for a poet." Petrarch idealizes nature and rural tranquility and praises the agreeableness of the country and the intimate satisfaction it offers the learned man who devotes himself to his garden and orchard.

Therefore, it was in the heart of the Euganean hills, among the lush green slopes, that the advantages and delights of villa life began to be appreciated, that the culture of the villa began to grow. Here was created that particular psychology that, over the following centuries would guide and inspire the aristocrats and literati, and would make the Venetian provinces richer, more fertile, and even more beautiful.

Petrarch's house, here seen with its vineyard, hidden in the ancient Euganean hills, represented the perfect solution to the humanists, who were trying to find in the countryside, the ideal place to dedicate themselves to learning, far from the confusion and stress of the city.

*Previous page: The
interior of Petrarch's
house, showing scenes from
Petrarch's life.*

*Petrarch's house. The
entrance hall with frescos
illustrating Petrarch's life.*

The poet's study.

Palazzo Da Mula

The Isle of Murano, Venice

In the centuries that followed the year 1000, Venice, that vital nucleus of trade and traffic, began to exercise an irresistible fascination. Soon a large throng of dwellings and *botteghe*, or shops, began to spring up around this commercial magnet, whilst the narrow winding canals became even more intricate and lively.

As soon as they had accumulated some money and discovered the pleasure of spending it, the busy merchants felt the need to get away from the bustling centre and find a little peace and tranquility in other parts of the lagoon. In the same period the diffusion of Petrachism and the humanistic culture manifested itself in a renewed love for nature, and of course, gardens.

And so the Giudecca was discovered. There one could relax in the peace of its fragrant orchards, which are clearly documented in Jacopo de Barbari's plan of 1500, where one can make out along the shores of the island, the beautiful Lombardesque façades of the villas, whose loggias and porticos opened out onto the gardens behind. One can also clearly see the courtyards with their wells, the vegetable gardens, the orchards, and the vineyards that almost completely cover the island.

Equally significant is a German engraving of the Cinquecento, depicting the delights of villa life on the Giudecca itself. In the courtyard of some wealthy dwelling several people in gorgeous clothes perform dances, whilst in the distance, beyond the wide St. Mark's Basin, one can see the Doge's Palace and the Basilica of St. Mark. More refined were those noble Venetians who chose as their ideal refuge the island of Murano. Alongside the glass furnaces – whose fumes were believed to purify the air – rose, from the end of the Quattrocento, splendid habitations, the first examples of a tradition that was to continue through the whole of the successive century. Some traces still remain of the frescos with which Paolo Veronese had decorated the rooms and façade of one patrician house, on which other illustrious exponents of Venetian art had also worked, namely Alessandro Vittoria and Vincenzo Scamozzi. But the golden period of Muranese houses (and by house I mean villa), was

without doubt the Quattrocento, when the top echelons of Venetian society, humanists and literati, magistrates of the Serenissima, patricians, and merchants settled on the island. It was here that the splendid palace of Caterina Cornaro, Queen of Cyprus arose, surrounded by a large garden, alongside the villas and palaces of the most illustrious dogal families of the city.

Of this refined humanistic climate, of this cultured and exclusive world, nothing, however, remains. On the island that is now densely populated, increasing numbers of dwellings have suffocated and invaded those orchards and gardens, which at one time characterized the physiognomy of the island, and gave rise to the saying *Murano è a Venezia molto simile ma vi si gode piu di amenitade* (Murano is much like Venice, but there one can enjoy the beauty more).

The last surviving architectural example of that glorious period is the Palazzo Da Mula, whose noble façade, elegantly embroidered with quadruple lancet windows, decorated Gothic balconies, and walls faced with costly marble reliefs, is reflected in the waters of the canals. Unfortunately, the interior decorations, the Gothic friezes, and the refined polychromes of the Renaissance decoration have all disappeared. But the garden still possesses a magnificent example of Byzantine art, a round-headed marble arch decorated with a band of exquisitely carved fantastic motifs.

Thus Palazzo Da Mula remains the only tangible memory of a particularly happy moment in Venetian history. In fact it was at Murano that the Venetian nobles and humanists enjoyed the tranquility of the surroundings, studying the ancient tracts on agriculture, and reading Petrarch's verses, nursing an increasing desire to get away from the city and its frenetic bustle. Murano witnessed the birth of a new psychology, a renewed appreciation and taste for villa life, that would inspire these Cinquecento Venetians to build their own country retreats overlooking the rivers and canals, and in every corner of the hinterland, in order to recapture and emulate the delights of these fragrant Muranese gardens.

Villa Dal Verme
Agugliaro, Vicenza

Villa dal Verme is an early example of the type of villa that was being built in Basso Vicentino in the fifteenth century. Its elegant Gothic façade used to be reflected in the waters of the Liona canal, but successive risings of the water level meant the construction of higher banks, which unfortunately now partially hide the villa.

Like the other fifteenth-century dwellings that still survive in Basso Vicentino, its origins seem to be irrevocably connected to the massive land reclamation schemes and canal building. These, since the thirteenth and fourteenth centuries, occupied the nobility and populace living in that vast plain that was embraced by the Berici and Euganean Hills.

This in fact was one of the areas that came under the supervision of the Magistrato ai Beni Inculti, who here carried out several important land reclamation schemes known as *retratti*. The Liona canal, for example, brought about the economic renaissance of this area, providing a rapid and safe means of communication to the markets.

It was the people of Vicenza who were first to realise the enormous possibilities of drainage schemes to salvage the arable land, at a time when the Serenissima Republic was still far more

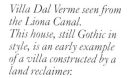

Villa Dal Verme seen from the Liona Canal.
This house, still Gothic in style, is an early example of a villa constructed by a land reclaimer.

involved in maritime commerce. So it was along the banks of the Liona, and the other rivers, threaded their way through Basso Vicentino, that there arose some of the oldest villas in the Veneto. The typology of Villa Dal Verme – the earliest example of decorated Gothic in the Vicenza countryside – is characteristic, that is, it is much more like a city palace than a rural dwelling.

However, as Ackermann says, we must not forget that the villa is "economically a satellite of the city," and this independence is emphasized, at least initially, by the same shared architectural forms that have been exported from the city into the country.

Even though Villa Dal Verme lacks agricultural outbuildings, it does possess the two large arches of the ground floor portico, which most probably responded to the needs of country life, acting as a sheltered landing place, a storehouse, and warehouse for the merchandise transported along the Liona waterway.

Villa Spessa

Carmignano di Brenta, Padua

Rarely does a place enjoy such good lines of communication as Villa Spessa does; at the meeting point of such important old Roman roads as the Postumia and near the only place where it is possible to ford the Brenta, it was obviously the perfect site for an important residence.

The villa was built for a certain Giovanni Andrea da Quinto, a middle class Cicentine who had made a lot of money in the wool business . He had begun, in the first quarter of the fifteenth century, to buy up the land around Spessa and Carmignano, which was excellent for sheep farming and, being well-watered, very suitable for the production of wool.

The confluence of the major communication routes and the nearness of the river Brenta explain the location of this majestic villa, whose owners were connected with the wool industry.

From an architectural point of view the building is very much like the palace of a noble citizen, in the Venetian style of the Quattrocento, but which here would form the centre of a proto-industrial estate. The Quinto family enjoyed a greater freedom of initiative here in respect to those regulations and limits that governed construction in the city, so they were able to put up a large building.

The construction still possessed, however, all the characteristics of a house equipped for practical and utilitarian exigencies. Only when it was purchased by the patrician Grimani in the sixteenth century did it acquire certain aspects of gentrification necessitated by a new, and more complex concept, of what a villa should represent.

The presence of a small chapel seems to support the hypothesis that a large number of workers' houses – probably built out of poor materials, for no trace remains today – had sprung up around this center of activity.

The façade of the small religious building demonstrates the clean forms of that Gothic style onto which Palladio would graft his own pure interpretations.

Detail of the façade, showing fifteenth-century decorations.

Villa Dall' Aglio

Lughignano di Casale sul Sile, Treviso

According to literary tradition, this villa was built by Caterina Cornaro and given as a wedding present to Fiammetta, who was one of her bridesmaids. Bembo tells the same story in his "Asolani." The building actually belongs to the late Quattrocento, even if some of the elegant capitals might tempt one to anticipate this dating by several decades.

As with Villa Agostini at Cusignana, the formula and typology is still that of a Venetian city dwelling. Here it has been ennobled by the perfect harmony of its forms and also by the elegant four-mullioned window, which adorns the main façade. The villa looks over the waters of the river Sile, a proximity that is by no means casual but is, in fact, due to precise needs.

As we have noted previously, villas were often built beside a river or canal, they were thus almost in symbiosis with the running water, which provided invaluable lines of communication and, in addition to this, a source of life for the surrounding countryside.

The portico and the façade that overlook the river Sile.

Villa Da Porto Colleoni

Thiene, Vicenza

Even though it is rather difficult to place Da Porto Colleoni castle in the logical development of the Venetian villa, this romantic building, with its noble proportions, is extremely interesting and must not be overlooked.

Generally believed to be one of the oldest examples of a castle-villa, it seems to be the result of a long series of modifications, additions, and reconstructions, which have not, however, diminished in any way from its evocative and highly original character. Apart from the varied construction work that took place between the fourteenth and nineteenth centuries, the sixteenth century saw the addition of the richly-painted frescos, where the festive and triumphant spirit of the Serenissima found its most immediate and admirable expression. Inside a *trompe l'oeil* loggia, frescos by Fasolo, and Zelotti portray various scenes from Roman history, such as Muzio Scevola, the meeting between Sophonisba and Massinissa, Anthony and Cleopatra, and the Clemency of Scipio.

The tripartite façade, the presence of two sturdy lateral towers, and a similar layout, all suggest certain parallels with the Fondaco dei Turchi, and more generally, with that typology of construction diffused over all the terra firma in the Quattrocento. The elegantly decorated, Gothic five-mullioned window, which graces the central portion of the complex, also adds weight to the impression that the building dates from the fifteenth century.

Like a typical medieval castle surrounded by walls and a moat, the complex includes a main dwelling-place, a small chapel, and other, more modest buildings.

Little, however, remains of its feudal and military character, for just beyond the castle walls there are the arcades of the villa, indicating the existence of a lifestyle no longer oppressed by medieval fears. Nevertheless, one can still sense a nostalgia for the days of knights and tournaments, a feeling that has not dulled or diminished over the centuries, for indeed it was just this type of fortified villa that inspired the Romantic architects of the nineteenth century.

A view of the castle showing the five-mullioned window and crenellations. Surrounded by a wall and flanked by sturdy towers, like the home of a warrior, the villa with its wide open loggias, established a more trusting relationship with nature.

Today the villa houses a most interesting collection of works by Maganza, Maffei, Pietro Vecchia, Langetti, and Boccacino.

The stables of villa Da Porto Colleoni, attributed to Francesco Muttoni.

*The large salon on the
ground floor, with frescos
by Giovanni Antonio
Fasolo and Giambattista
Zelotti.*

*Giovanni Antonio Fasolo
and Giambattista Zelotti;
The Clemency of
Scipio.*

Giambattista Zelotti
(1526–1578)

Giambattista Zelotti was one of the most famous and highly-praised fresco painters in the Veneto in the middle of the sixteenth century. Born in Verona in 1526, he collaborated with Paolo Veronese on the frescos of Villa Da Porto Colleoni at Thiene and of Villa Soranza, as well as at Venice, in the Doge's Palace (1553–1554) and in the Libreria (1556–1557). He was also active in Vicenza, in the Palazzo Chiericati (1558) and in the Duomo (1572), and was much in demand among the nobility of that time, who often entrusted to him the decoration of their country houses. In about 1557 he completed the enormous cycle of frescos at Villa Godi at Lonedo; later he worked at Villa Emo at Fanzolo and also at the Malcontenta. In the early 1570s we find him at the castle of Catajo at Battaglia, and in the rooms of the Villa Caldogno at Caldogno. In 1572 he completed the frescos of Villa Porto at Torri di Quartesolo. In 1575 he moved to Mantova, where he was Prefect of the ducal buildings, and where he died in 1578.

Villa Da Porto Colleoni, the large salon, showing scenes from the Clemency of Scipio by Antonio Fasolo and Giambattista Zelotti; at either side of the fireplace there are frescos by Giovanni Antonio Fasolo portraying Vulcan and Venus.

Giovanni Antonio Fasolo
(1530–1572)

The amusements, the pastimes, and the delights of villa life found, in the Cinquecento, a careful and sensitive interpreter in the person of Giovanni Antonio Fasolo. Born at Modello, on lake Como, in 1530, he went to Vincenza when he was still only a boy. He collaborated with Paolo Veronese on the Venetian church of San Sebastiano (1556) and was later commissioned to carry out the decorations for the Teatro Olimpico (1557–1602) and for the Loggia del Capitanio (1568) at Vicenza, a city where he often worked. He is especially well known for his frescos in the numerous villas of the province of Vicenza and the neighboring areas. In 1555, together with Zelotti, he painted several scenes in the large salon of Villa Da Porto Colleoni at Thiene. Around 1560 he frescoed the open gallery of Villa Roberti at Brugine, and, several years later, worked at Albettone, in the home of the Capiglia family, where part of his important work can still be seen today; and lastly, during the 1570s, he was working on the enormous cycle of frescos at Villa Calgogno at Caldogno, which proved in fact, to be his last work. Fasolo died at Vicenza in 1572.

Villa Giustinian

Roncade, Treviso

The walls of the ancient castle guard the open architecture of the villa, almost as if to emphasize the transformation that has taken place, over the centuries, in the home of a nobleman.

A grandiose architectural complex of the early Cinquecento, Villa Giustinian's special fascination derives from the double physiognomy that characterizes it.

From the outside it looks like a severe medieval castle, with its crenellations, moat, and massive protective curtain wall with its sturdy corner towers. However, despite this forbidding appearance, it is not in fact a feudal nucleus surviving from the days before the Serenissima annexed the hinterland, instead it is a peaceful country residence constructed by Girolamo Giustinian in this way to perpetuate the memory of the ancient home of the Sanzi family.

Therefore, to quote J. S. Ackerman, these types of architectural form are "expressions of power and aspirations of class," that for their symbolic value can coexist with "an avantegarde villa of the early Cinquecento," which is how he describes Villa Giustinian.

As soon as one passes over the fake drawbridge, the dark medieval atmosphere quickly disappears, and in the center of this fortified space we can see a majestic villa, one of the most emblematical architectural expressions on the Venetian terra firma. No longer a closed, inward-looking, defensive structure created in the Middle Ages, but a surprising opening of porticos and airy loggias, an original interpretation of that "open architecture," which for centuries had characterized Venetian buildings, and which, once peace had been restored, would be found all over the hinterland.

A rare example of Lombardesque architecture, Villa Giustinian is made even more beautiful by the delightful pastel-colored frescos that decorate its façade. With its cordial open porticos it predates Palladio's ingenious inventions by several decades.

Villa Giustinian, the
sturdy watch towers
flanking the fake
drawbridge.

The elegant, arched
Lombardesque loggia
superimposed on the façade
of the villa.

Queen Caterina Cornaro's Barco
Altivole, Treviso

When the Prince of Lusignano died, his wife, Caterina Cornaro, inherited the dominion of Cyprus. Her reign, however, was short. Venice, fully aware of the island's strategic importance and considering the continuous attacks to which it was subject, entered into discussions with the Queen, and in 1489 finally convinced her to renounce her sovreignty. In exchange she was given the Signoria of Asolo, which she kept until her death in 1510.

After having lived in a sumptuous palace in Cyprus, Caterina was obviously not going to be too happy with either of her Asolan residences, the one an austere castle on top of the hill, and the other a modest little palace in the middle of town; her ambitions were far grander, and her culture much more refined.

So it was in 1490, soon after arriving in Asolo, that she started the construction of a magnificent villa at Altivole, built to the designs of Piero Lugato, where she realized her humanistic dreams, and where art vied with nature to satisfy every longing for spectacular views, color, shade, and fragrance. The extensive estate was watered by many small rivers and streams, tributaries of the Piave, which not only irrigated the fields, kitchen gardens, and orchards but supplied water for the elegant fountains and for the elaborate water jokes, which were used at parties to catch out the unsuspecting guests.

So, at Altivole two different lifestyles existed contemporaneously; alongside that of the agrarian world, with its seasonal labors, harvests, crops, and fruits, there was that of the court, a gay and carefree world, inspired by its humanistic love of nature.

The noble residence of Caterina is still known by the name "Barco" – a word which Bembo used to signify "Paradise" – and it was in this paradise, this delightful retreat, that the Queen loved to surround herself with her elect court of artists and literati. It was the same Bembo who was so enchanted with the town and its inhabitants, that he invented the word *asolare*, which means to pass one's days surrounded by the beauty of nature. The receptions, elegant banquets, and elaborate amusements that were consolation for the loss of her island kingdom, seem to be strangely echoed in the stupendous xylographs that illustrate the *Hypnerotomachia Poliphili*. An allegorical romance, interwoven with subtle symbolism and literary references, the "Poliphilo" was the perfect answer to the dreams and cultural aspirations of the late Quattrocento; with its descriptions of gardens, orchards and viridaria, of fountains and elegant architecture, it represented a humanistic celebration of beauty, and extolled the most cultured and refined customs of villa life.

Unfortunately, hardly anything remains of the Barco of Altivole, which, if it had been conserved in its entirety, would have without doubt constituted the most remarkable example of Quattrocento architecture in the Venetian countryside. It was not long before it embarked on its slow and gradual process of degradation and deterioration, and in 1831 the last towers and crumbling buildings were torn down, and the fountain eventually found its way to a museum in Vienna.

Only the words of Bembo and the haunting images of the *Poliphilo* remain to testify to the amazing beauty and vastness of the complex; the only surviving architectural testimony of that exquisite and festive world is the elegant Lombardesque loggia, in Nanto stone, which flanked the main building in much the same way as occurs in Venetian houses.

Polyphilus kneels in reverence before the throne of Queen Eleuterillide, surrounded by her court (Francesco Colonna, Hypnerotomachia Poliphili *Venice, 1499).*

The character of the painted decorations on the loggia is surprisingly conservative, especially that of the Oratorium, where the inspiration seems to belong to a tradition and culture far removed from the splendors and pastimes that blossomed at the Court of the Queen of Cyprus. Theater historians believe that the great Ruzante himself recited his works in this loggia in the summer of 1521.

Recently a monument has been erected in the center of Altivole, in front of the church, to another personage who had a very important role in the history of the Venetian villas – Fra' Giocondo, the great Veronese architect, protagonist of many official building projects undertaken by Serenissima, both in the field of hydraulic engineering and civic construction. The monument to Fra' Giocondo in this very place is very apt, and fits in well with the memory of the villa that Caterina Cornaro was building in those same years.

Both the architect and the Queen were inspired by the highest standards of culture and learning, and both were protagonists in one of the most memorable and fascinating periods in the history of the villa.

Garden with the fountain of Venus; Polia makes a laurel wreath for Poliphilus: (Francesco Colonna, Hypnerotomachia Poliphili, *Venice, 1499).*

All that is left of Caterina Cornaro's famous villa, the Barco, mentioned in the Poliphilo *by Fra Giocondo and by Pietro Bembo, is this wonderful Lombardesque loggia.*

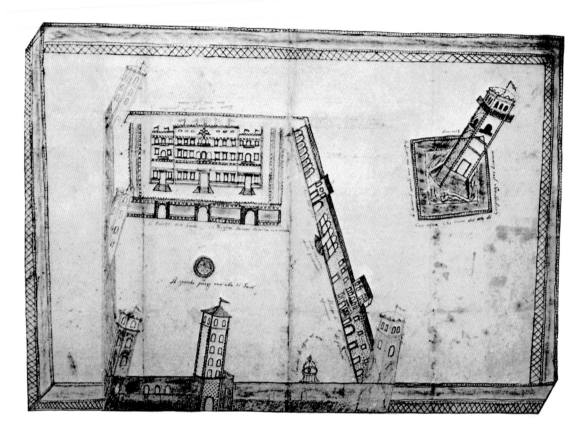

Plan of Caterina Cornaro's villa at Altivole, a drawing from the seventeenth century (Asolo, Civil Museum).

Barco of the Queen Caterina Cornaro, a fifteenth-century loggia with traces of elaborate frescoed decorations, and a detail of a capital.

Palazzo alla Corte, known as "Villa Ottavia"

La Costa di Rovolon, Padua

This building, which is now known as Villa Ottavia, is at Rovolon, on those slopes of the Euganean hills that look out onto the setting sun. Here we have a page of history that is of exceptional importance, and closely linked to the development of the Venetian villas.

It must not be forgotten that the Paduan Benedictine Order was chiefly concerned with the countryside rather than with the city, instigating well-organized agricultural projects, and more important, extensive land reclamation schemes. Naturally here they worked together with the Paduan and Venetian nobles until the Magistrato dei beni inculti assumed the definitive systemization of the territory.

In 970 Bishop Gauslino had endowed the monastery of Santa Giustina in Padua with extensive lands, which included several churches, and amongst these was the church of San Giorgio in Rovolon. More land in the same area was purchased in 1441, and this included the hamlet of La Costa with the houses of Giovanni Parisino, where at one time had existed a fortress belonging to the Counts of Padua.

The Rector had his residence and administrative offices here, in the Palazzo alla "Corte," whilst another functionary acted as official at the "Corte del Vegrolongo" in the neighborhood of Bastia, where the monks owned another 700 fields.

At the "Court of Rovolon," in the 1500s, the monks collected the rents and the tithes – the half and tenth part of the grain, the third and tenth part of the vegetables, the half and tenth part of the wine "brought in grapes to press at the Court of Vegrolongo."

Angelo Portenari, in his book *Della Felicità di Padova* (1623) talks about the hill of Rovolon, "which towards the west is planted with vines and trees, and which has a gracious outlook over the plain," and the places which "have by the same

monks been embellished and made very beautiful, and for delightfulness can be compared with any place near Padua."

Apropos this last remark, it is interesting to know that the Palace of Rovolon, with its marvelous setting, was also used as a country retreat for the monks from the abbey at Padua, and in fact this is still the function of the ancient palace today.

The main body of the building, which echoes the typical style of the Venetian house, is embellished by an elegant portico, providing access to the villa and to the open Lombardesque loggia that overlooks the valley.

Villa dei Vescovi
Luvigliano di Torreglia, Padua

Giovanni Maria Falconetto
(1468–ca. 1540)

Giovanni Maria Falconetto, an architect and painter born at Verona in 1468, had an important influence on the development of the villa in the Veneto. The first phase of his artistic career was dedicated essentially to frescos, and he worked in the church of Saints Nazaro and Celso (1497–1499) and in the Calcasoli chapel at Verona. After moving to Padua in order to be able to enjoy the patronage of Alvise Cornaro, he distinguished himself as an architect, designing the Loggia and the Odeon (1524) for his patron, and the city gates of San Giovanni (1528) and Savonarola (1530). Again for Cornaro he built the Villa dei Vescovi at Luvigliano, one of the first examples of Venetian architecture to be inspired by Ancient Rome. He also designed Villa Cornaro at Este, of which only the triumphal Arch, built of Nanto stone, remains. The actual date of his death is uncertain, but it took place around the year 1540.

Villa dei Vescovi, designed by Giovanni Maria Falconetto in the heart of the Euganean hills.

Before Palladio's ideals regarding the design and construction of villas spread around the Venetian hinterland, the country residences were of a very varied physiognomy, being the result of the owner's wishes and, of course, influenced by the presence of existing architecture.

This was the situation at Luvigliano, where in 1529, Giovanni Maria Falconetto was commissioned by the Bishop of Padua to build a summer residence on the foundations of a medieval castle. Falconetto received the commission through the devices of his friend and patron, Alvise Cornaro, who was the administrator of Pisani, the Bishop of Padua.

Situated in an open valley in the form of an amphitheater, deep in the heart of the Euganean hills, the Veronese architect built the princely residence on different levels, its massive rectangular structure is relieved by the sudden and unexpected openings of porticos and loggias.

The whole complex possesses a sense of noble monumentality; the elegant balustrades, the turns of the wide steps that connect the various floors, the walled courtyard with its classic arcades, are all elements of Falconetto's particular conception of a villa.

Built of the materials from the ruins of the castle, the villa has a most charming and elegant interior. All the rooms are frescoed with floral motifs and refined Mannerist mythological groups executed in brilliant colors, the work perhaps of Lambert Sustris, a Flemish painter.

Without doubt Cornaro's presence was very important in the history of this villa, both as administrator of the Bishop and friend of the architect: "And if a gentleman or private person desires to know how to build in the city, come to the Cornaro house in Padua; if he wants to build a villa, go to Codevigo and to Campagna; he who wants to build a palace worthy of a prince, must go to Luvigliano."

All of the above mentioned buildings were by Falconetto. Although the palace at Luvigliano had little resonance in the Veneto and is of no consequence in the history of the Venetian villas, it nevertheless represents a particular cultural moment; what prevails is that triumphant Roman spirit, which was to influence the architecture of Sanmicheli, if not Palladio.

110

*The Euganean Hills seen
through the arch of the
loggia of Villa dei Vescovi.*

*Interior of the villa with
frescos by Lamberto
Sustris.*

Villa Garzoni
Pontecasale di Candiana, Padua

When, in the fifteenth century, Venice had triumphantly conquered the terra firma, many estates belonging to the local nobility were appropriated by the Serenissima and then auctioned off to the highest bidder. This was to be the fate of 1500 fields of the estate owned by the Dal Verme family at Pontecasale. Put up for sale in 1440, the land was purchased by one Luigi Garzoni, a member of a very wealthy Venetian banking family.

One hundred years later, evidently inspired or stimulated by the general climate of patriotic fervor, the Garzoni family undertook various land reclamation and drainage projects, and eventually, as by now was the custom, commissioned the construction of an important residence, destined to be a symbol or expression of the family's wealth and prestige.

The major artists working at Venice at that time were consulted and the task of designing the building was entrusted to the famous Jacopo Tatti, known as Sansovino, who as Vasari writes: "Made the palace of Signor Luigi de Garzoni longer than the Fondaco dei Turchi, on every side, by thirteen paces, and with much comfort, for the water runs all through the palace, which is adorned with four very beautiful figures by Sansovino, the said palace

Symbolic example of the villa of a land reclaimer; this large imposing white building proclaims the wealth of the Garzoni family, who initiated a series of land reclamation projects in the area.

Villa Godi
Lonedo di Lugo, Vicenza

Villa Godi, whose severe form dominates the beautiful rolling foothills of the Dolomites, is one of Palladio's first documented works. Dating from just before his Roman experiences, Villa Godi seems to be imprinted with a profoundly Venetian style. It could be seen as a sixteenth-century reproposal of the traditional twin-towered house that was built all over the province of Vicenza during the fifteenth century. The structurally unitary construction of the various parts, which would later be typical of Palladio, are still only in an embryonic state here, and the central spine of the villa seems to be inserted rather than integrated into the building.

Illustrated in the *Quattro Libri*, Villa Godi is a large construction with two tower-like blocks which convey a sense of strength and solidarity. Ackerman describes it as an example of a centralized cubic villa, "which is in clear contradiction with nature." And it does, in fact, lack that cordial rapport which usually existed between Palladio's villas and their environment. The building is surrounded by a large park (which was landscaped in the nineteenth century by Antonio Caregaro Negrin) and seems to clearly express the ambitions and prestige of its *committente*, Girolamo Godi, who, as Palladio notes, spared no expense in order to achieve a perfection of form.

The entrance to the house is particularly interesting. A steep flight of steps, enclosed by two projecting wings, leads up to a balustrade balcony, which in turn leads into a tripartite portico.

The interior of Villa Godi is in complete contrast to the exterior, and seems like the inside of a jewel casket, richly and even sumptuously decorated. Indeed, some of the foremost fresco painters of the time worked here, artists such as Gualtiero, Padovano, Giambattista Zelotti and Battista del Moro who filled the various rooms and the belvedere loggia with an exuberance of figures, scenes and decorations which sometimes seems excessive. Whole walls are hidden beneath caryatids and *trompe l'oeil* columns, classical scenes, mythological figures or military triumphs, or else they open up like windows on to the vast and luminous

Andrea Palladio.
Description, plan and
elevation of Villa Godi at
Lonedo. (I Quattro Libri
dell' Architecttura,
Vence, 1570, book II
chapter XV).

IN LONEDO luogo del Vicentino è la feguente fabrica del Signor Girolamo de' Godi pofta fopra vn colle di bellifsima uifta,& a canto un fiume,che ferue per Pefchiera. Per rendere quefto
fito commodo per l'vfo di Villa ui fono ftati fatti cortili, & ftrade fopra uolti con non picciola fpefa.
La fabrica di mezo è per l'habitatione del padrone, & della famiglia. Le ftanze del padrone hanno
il piano loro alto da terra tredici piedi, e fono in folaro, fopra quefte ui fono i granari, & nella parte di
fotto, cioè nell'altezza de i tredeci piedi ui fono difpofte le cantine,i luoghi da fare i uini, la cucina,
& altri luoghi fimili. La Sala giugne con la fua altezza fin fotto il tetto, & ha due ordini di feneftre.
Dall'vno e l'altro lato di quefto corpo di fabrica ui fono i cortili, & i coperti per le cofe di Villa. E'
ftata quefta fabrica ornata di pitture di bellifsima inuentione da Meffer Gualtiero Padouano,da Mef
fer Battifta del Moro Veronefe, & da Meffer Battifta Venetiano ; perche quefto Gentil'huomo, ilquale è giudiciofifsimo, per redurla a quella eccellenza & perfettione,che fia pofsibile ; non ha guar
dato a fpefa alcuna,& ha fcelto i più fingolari, & eccellenti Pittori de' noftri tempi.

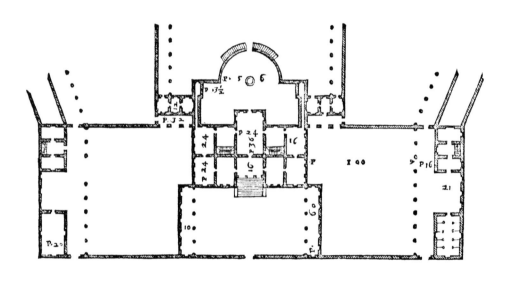

trompe l'oeil landscapes of Gualtiero Padovano, as if to capture forever an idealized rapport with nature. Trophies of war and various allegories complete the decorations, and one can make out the noble figure of Securitas, an obvious reference and celebration of the peace finally achieved after the dark and terrible period of the War of Cambrai, after which it was once more feasible and possible to build villas in every corner of the Venetian countryside.

Andrea Palladio
(1508–1580)

Undisputed protagonist of the history and culture of the Venetian villas, Andrea Palladio, born in Padova in 1508, began his career as a stone dresser, first in the Paduan workshop of Bartolomeo Cavassa da Sossano, and later at Vicenza. Here, in about 1540, he met Giangiorgio Trissino, who became his patron and introduced him into cultured and aristocratic circles. In 1542 he won a competition to construct a two-storey loggia round old Palazzo della Ragione, referred to since his time as the Basilica, which contributed greatly to the spread of his fame as an architect. He thus obtained the commission to build several public buildings, amongst which was the Loggia of the Capitanio at Vicenza, as well as many private buildings. Palladio knew how to interpret and realize the expectations and the ideals of the nobles of the time who asked him to design their city palaces and country villas. Ingenious inventor of the Teatro Olimpico, passionate student of the classical world, Palladio is also famous for his treatise on architecture published in Venice in 1570. Less frequent were his exploits in the field of religious buildings; in Venice he designed the church of S. Giorgio Maggiore and the Redentore, and his last work before his death in 1580 was the Tempietto at Maser.

The loggia of the villa with frescos by Gualtiero Padovano overlooks the garden and the surrounding hills. The cycle of frescos inside the building were carried out between the years 1552 and 1553 and represent the first example of villa decoration conceived on a larger scale.

Villa Godi, Salon of
Olympus, with frescos by
Giambattista Zelotti,
portraying the gods of
Olympus who appear in
the sky above the ruins of a
Greek temple.

Salon of Venus, frescos by Giambattista Zelotti; the scene portrays Euralius and Niso; two figures peer out from a trompe l'oeil door; anticipating the realistic figures at Villa Emo, Maser.

Villa Pisani
Bagnolo di Lonigo, Vicenza

Not far from Lonigo, at the point where the old Roman road crosses the river Guà, there stands the severe façade of the Palladian Villa Pisani. Signors of the surrounding territory, a wealthy family made even wealthier by their organized agricultural activities and by their introduction of specialized cultivation, the Pisanis had already had a palace, which is now the town hall, built for them at Lonigo. They now thought it was necessary to have a place in the country, on their estate, a dwelling with ample store-houses, granaries and other agricultural buildings which would form the nucleus of their agricultural operations. Palladio was thus asked to design a complex which would not only be functional and practical, but which would also convey a sense of authority and prestige suitable to the feudal power which the Pisani exercised over Lonigo and the surrounding area.

The villa, built in an area which already bore the traces of many ancient settlements, manages to preserve the memory of the pre-existing medieval castle, with its two stocky towers and ashlar-work which, as Ackerman points out, still manages to signify a military or public function, whilst from the river it appears almost to be a triumphal arch.

The classical portico of the rear elevation, shown in the *Quattro Libri* but unfortunately never completed, was to have opened out onto the rear courtyard, almost as if to celebrate the establishment of Renaissance culture in the countryside.

The enormous agricultural wings formed the nucleus of the Pisani's intense agricultural activity and flourishing commerce. Before they were destroyed by wartime events, these agricultural wings, spanned by never-ending Doric colonnades, were said to have enclosed a space as big as St. Mark's Square.

Palladio remarks that the large salon on the piano nobile is inspired by a Roman house. It was here where the Pisanis, as representatives of the Serenissima, carried out their public duties.

Frescos of allegorical groups decorate the main salon, whilst in another room on the same floor there are traces of frescos portraying the delights and amusements of life in a villa.

Built by Andrea Palladio on the bank of the navigable canal and center of an enormous agricultural estate, this villa, with its magnificent triumphal arch, proclaims the authority and prestige of the Pisani family. The Roman classical and Mannerist inspirations, noticeable in the ashlar-work of the arches, the semi-circular steps, and the pediment, marry well with the traditional Venetian dovecotes, an example of Palladio's constant search for beauty combined with usefulness.

Andrea Palladio. Description, plan and view of Villa Pisani di Bagnolo I Quattro Libri dell'Architettura, *Venice, 1570, book II, chapter XIV).*

L A F A B R I C A, che fegue è in Bagnolo luogo due miglia lontano da Lonigo Ca
ftello del Vicentino, & è de' Magnifici Signori Conti Vittore, Marco, e Daniele fra
telli de' Pifani. Dall'vna, e l'altra parte del cortile ui fono le ftalle, le cantine, i granari, e fimili altri luoghi per l'ufo della Villa. Le colonne de i portici fono di ordine Dorico. La parte di mezo di quefta fabrica è per l'habitatione del Padrone: il
pauimento delle prime ftanze è alto da terra fette piedi: fotto ui fono le cucine, &
altri fimili luoghi per la famiglia. La Sala è in uolto alta quanto larga, e la metà più: à quefta altezza
giugne ancho il uolto delle loggie: Le ftanze fono in folaro alte quanto larghe: le maggiori fono lun
ghe un quadro e due terzi: le altre un quadro e mezo. Et è da auertirfi che non fi ha hauuto molta
confideratione nel metter le fcale minori in luogo, che habbiano lume viuo (come habbiamo ricor-
dato nel primo libro) perche non hauendo effe à feruire, fe non à i luoghi di fotto, & à quelli di fopra,
i quali feruono per granari ouer mezati; fi ha hauuto rifguardo principalmente ad accommodar be-
ne l'ordine di mezo: il quale è per l'habitatione del Padrone, e de' foreftieri: e le Scale, che à queft'or
dine portano; fono pofte in luogo attifsimo, come fi uede ne i difegni. E ciò farà detto ancho per
auertenza del prudente lettore per tutte le altre fabriche feguenti di un'ordine folo: percioche in
quelle, che ne hanno due belli, & ornati; ho curato che le Scale fiano lucide, e pofte in luoghi commo
di: e dico due; perche quello, che uà fotto terra per le cantine, e fimili ufi, e quello che uà nella parte
di fopra, e ferue per granari, e mezati non chiamo ordine principale, per non darfi all'habitatione de'
Gentil'huomini.

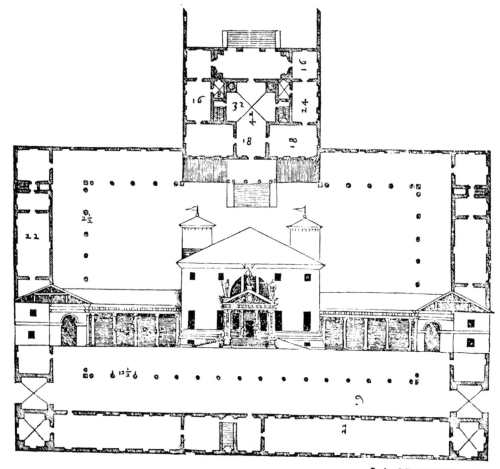

LA SEGVENTE

*Villa Pisani. Main salon,
with thermal window and
painted decoration from
the fifteenth century.*

133

Villa Pojana
Pojana Maggiore, Vicenza

Palladio's plans for Villa Pojana manage to answer two basically different needs. On the one hand he conveys the old military traditions of the owner's family, and on the other their comparatively recent but very intense interest in agriculture.

Highly distinguished in the arts of war and totally faithful to the Serenissima whatever the emergency, the Pojana family had for centuries exercised a jurisdiction that was almost feudal over the surrounding area, and this powerful military background is expressed by the severity and austere purity of the villa built by Palladio for Bonifacio Pojana in the years 1548–1549. It was not only the family that enjoyed military connections, but the whole area, which had for many years supplied the Venetian army with its cavalry.

However, with the arrival of more peaceful times and with the renewed enthusiasm for what Alvise Cornaro called "blessed agriculture," also the Pojana began to discover the joys and benefits of their country estate.

They now became involved in the land, just as Marcus Billienus, a Roman centurion from the battle of Azio who is mentioned on a stone tablet found at Pojana, had done centuries before.

Wigh Villa Pojana, which is slightly elevated and so well proportioned as to seem smaller than it really is, Palladio's spirit of synthesis appears to have achieved its maximum expression: a Roman serliana dominates the façade, whilst beautifully simple linear pilasters support the pierced arch.

Palladio himself documented the "interior decorations" by Bernardino India, Anselmo Canera and Bartolomeo Ridolfi. In the atrium, elegant stucco frames, whose floral designs entwine around *trompe l'oeil* reliefs, enclose monochromes of river gods, while here and there appear patches of sky populated with other deities. The bust of Bonifacio Pojana looks down from over the main entrance, and above him are the family's coat of arms and military trophies.

Other decorations depict Pompeian scenes with the backgrounds and landscapes strewn with picturesque ruins and broken columns, whilst monochromatic figures of warriors stand watch in the *trompe l'oeil* niches. The most significant fresco of all can be found in the central hall: a family from classical times, dressed in tunics and togas, kneel in front of an altar whilst the paterfamilias extinguishes the torch of war at the feet of the statue of Peace which stands on the altar. It is a clear allusion to that peace so painstakingly and painfully achieved, which would finally allow the Venetians to enjoy the delights of the terra firma.

Palladio brilliantly interpreted the old military traditions of the Pojana family, and their more recent interest in agriculture, in his masterpiece at Pojana, where Bramantesque and Mannerist touches, such as the serliana and divided pediment, combine together to produce a design of sheer purity.

Anonymous design inspired by the Nymphaeum of Genazzano by Donato Bramante, clearly related to the Palladian motif of the double lintel enclosing the five oculi in the façade of Villa Pojana (Florence, Uffizi, Arch 4).

The villa seen through the main gateway.

On the following pages: The façade of Villa Pojana, emphasized by the squared openings of the windows and with the very interesting central serliana.

Palazzo Chiericati

Vicenza

A building designed to express prestige and nobility. Constructed at the entrance to the city near the ancient quay of the Bacchiglione, this Palladian palace seems to repropose the typology of the "maritime villa" often found in classical scenes. The motif of the internal courtyard with its porticos and loggias typical of Palladian palaces, is here moved to the façade, with the uninterrupted repetition of columns, just halted on the second floor; where there are the windows of the main reception rooms.

Perhaps the positioning of the chapter dealing with Palazzo Chiericati in the *Quattro Libri* is not merely casual: one of the last palaces built in the city of Vicenza, it comes immediately before the section devoted to villa construction. In effect the elevation, with its double orders of colonnades and multiple openings which involve the external space, seems to be a reproposal of the ideal villa of the classical world. The man who commissioned the building was Girolamo Chiericati, a member of that "generation of the great Utopia" who frequently turned to Palladio to interpret and realize their own ideals.

One of the supervisors of the loggia of the Basilica, Chiericati was to enjoy a close and fruitful friendship with Andrea Palladio. Encouraged by the prevailing climate of euphoria and high ideals, they collaborated on the ambitious project of requalifying urbanistically the big empty area known as the "Isola," decentered with respect to the traditional "magnets" of the city, not cluttered by any medieval buildings, in fact just a wide open space. This was obviously the ideal site for Chiericati's new palace, creating a new architectonic nucleus from which one could structure and organize the whole area. Several important buildings rose up in rapid succession (the Cogollo house, the Teatro Olimpico and the Palazzo Piovene) and this was also the place where the lines of communication between Venice and Vicenza, and Padova and Vicenza met, both by road – crossing the Ponte degli Angeli (also by Palladio) – and by water, by means of the Bacchiglione.

The Pianta Angelica clearly shows the presence of a city gate in this area; so from the wide porticos and loggias of the Palazzo Chiericati one could watch the arrival of the boats from Venice, which, from time to time drew out the authorities and the Vicenza populace to welcome the new captains, to watch the embarkation of the press-gang and to comment on the latest political and social news.

So as it stood at such an important and busy place, the Palazzo Chiericati was also designed to represent and express the "civilized face" of the

Villa Badoer
Fratta Polesine, Rovigo

One of the most precious and beautifully conserved of all Palladian villas is in the small town of Fratta, which lies in the Polesan plan. This expanse of land was the object of many reclamation and drainage schemes, as can be seen by the numerous rivers and canals which thread their way across the fields. It was here, in the middle of this rich and fertile plain, on the land which they had salvaged from the swamps, that the Badoer commissioned Palladio to build them a country residence.

With its harmonious proportions, Villa Badoer is arranged around a small circular courtyard: the main body of the house and the two amazingly elegant curved wings of the outbuildings are complemented by the rhythmic movement of the colonnades, which confer a noble yet restrained beauty to the whole complex. Here we do not find the majestic structure of some of the other Palladian villas, as it lacks the usual symbols of prestige and *sacralità*, such as cupolas, pinnacles, and akroterion statues. Here, instead, their place has been taken by simplicity, by refined harmony and sober elegance. Similarly, the agricultural wings of Villa Badoer cannot be compared with the agricultural wings of other Palladian villas,

Villa Barbaro
Maser, Treviso

The history of the Venetian villas takes up an entire chapter in the history of architecture, as do the Greek temples, the chatêaus of the Loire, and the skyscrapers of New York. And the name which occurs most often in this chapter is naturally that of Andrea Palladio.

Whenever wars cease and that sense of tranquility which is produced by a feeling of wellbeing starts to be diffused, this is the moment when man builds villas in the country, on the hills, along the banks of the rivers, beside lakes, near the sea. The many and different waves of this phenomenon can be counted and are easily recognizable, for they all share one constant factor the presence, either more or less direct or conscious, of ancient Rome. "Venetia" – as Andrea Palladio wrote in his preface to his *Quattro Libri*, – "is the sole remaining example of the grandeur and magnificence of the Romans."

The aristocratic Venetians, reading Cato, Columella, Varrone, and any other author who had written about classical agriculture and whose works were being willingly reprinted by wise Venetian publishers, knew very well that the villas they were planning to build had to be in proportion to the enormous area of arable or cultivated land which surrounded them. This was not true just for the volume of agricultural work, but also for the actual organism of the estate, so the villa became the element of synthesis which was necessary to demonstrate the extent of their possessions.

The owners of the Venetian villas, noblemen and farmers at the same time, were men who had attained the highest level of human dignity, who are not only known through history and literature, but also by the portraits painted of them by Titian, Vittoria, and other artists of Cinquecento Venice. As Palladio claimed, the villas resemble their owners, they are in fact portraits. "If you want to know the character and mind of the owner, observe with attention how he has built his house" – so reads an inscription on the wall of a villa near Vicenza.

Many Venetian clients had the good fortune to find in Andrea Palladio an architect who knew how to interpret and realize their dreams of

Jacopo Sansovino. Presumed portrait of Andrea Palladio (Venice, St. Mark's Sacristy, detail of bronze door).

culture and glory in a concrete way. The quintessence of his poetry had its roots in Padua, the city of Alvise Cornaro, in the classical culture and in an intellectual structure based on *esperientia*, which leads to *scientia*, which in turn leads to the study of those mysterious laws which govern the harmony of the world. At that moment a new ethic was born, no longer bound by medieval constraints and inhibitions, man now exulted in himself, considered himself capable of wonderful things: "He must strive to imitate in his creations," as Ackerman says, "the supreme rational order which permeates the divine creation."

During his visit to Rome Palladio was continuously stimulated not only by the ancient monuments and ruins, which he sketched and measured, but also by the buildings designed by Bramante, Raphael, and Michelangelo. His personality, however, remained independent and autonomous, and, we may add, completely Venetian. He was an ideal citizen at that magic and exhilarating moment following the Peace of Bologna (1529–30) when, Florence and Romes having collapsed, the city on the lagoon reached the apex of its splendor. Just as sumptuous palaces rose up along the sides of the Grand Canal, so in the countryside, reclaimed and salvaged by the Venetian and local landowners, arose the splendid villas of the great Venetian families of the aristocracy, of the rich merchants and soldiers of fortune, and of the humanists and men of the church. The habit of spending a long time in the country to administer one's estates united them in their ideals and needs, of which Palladio would be their interpreter.

The most famous and well preserved of the Venetian villas is that which the Barbaro brothers had built for them at Maser, near Asolo, in the heart of the Marca Trevigiana. Not far from Altivole, where one could still see Caterina Cornaro's Barco, is the hill where the Barnaros chose to construct their home. It is neither at the top of the hill, nor at the bottom, but halfway down the gentle slope, and the peaceful atmosphere makes one think of a landscape by the school of Giorgione. One could even say that the architectonic and decorative example provided by Villa Barbaro represents the synthesis of all the ideals of the Venetian culture on the terra firma in the sixteenth century.

The grandiose complex was designed for Marc'Antonio and Daniele Barbaro, sons of Francesco who, besides leaving an enormous patrimony, had had the idea of creating a type of monument at Maser for his descendants, and this explains why his name as well as those of his sons appears on the front of the villa. Daniele and Marc'Antonio had evidently formed a *fraterna* in order to keep the family fortune intact, but entrusting the administration to the elder son, who also had the task of providing an heir to secure the continuation of the line. The first son, Marc'Antonio, Procurator of San Marco de Supra, had served as the Republic's Ambassador to France, Constantinople, and England. He had also held the post of Procurator of the Arsenale and of "Proveditore al Sale," a man of great importance in the public life of Venice. His brother Daniele was, instead, a man of the church of science and of culture. Asked by the Republic to assume the Patriarchate of Aquilea, he took part in the Council of Trent in 1562–1563, but cultural

obligations always took precedence over political and religious ones.

Friends of artists and literati, from Bembo to Alvise Cornaro, from Varchi to Della Casa and Sperone Speroni, and painted by Paolo Veronese, Daniele Barbaro had not only published the *Pratica della prospettiva* and other studies, but also the translation and commentary of Vitruvius' *Trattato*, whose illustrations were by Andrea Palladio.

We have mentioned the political activities of the Barbaro brothers, and earlier in the book we talked a little about the Cinquecento notion that a villa resembled its owner well, even though it may be true that at Maser there is the constant presence of Marc'Antonio, the villa bears an even closer resemblance to Daniele, who as we remember was

Paolo Veronese. Portrait of Daniele Barbaro, on the table the Libri dell'Architettura, *the result of the collaboration of this noble scholar with Palladio, (Amsterdam, Rijksmuseum).*

LA SOTTOPOSTA fabrica è à Maſera Villa vicina ad Aſolo Caſtello del Triuigiano, di Monſignor Reuerendiſsimo Eletto di Aquileia, e del Magnifico Signor Marc'Antonio fratelli de' Barbari. Quella parte della fabrica, che eſce alquanto in fuori; ha due ordini di ſtanze, il piano di quelle di ſopra è à pari del piano del cortile di dietro, ouc è tagliata nel monte rincontro alla caſa vna fontana con infiniti ornamenti di ſtucco, e di pittura. Fa queſta fonte vn laghetto, che ſerue per peſchiera: da queſto luogo partitaſi l'acqua ſcorre nella cucina, & dapoi irrigati i giardini, che ſono dalla deſtra, e ſiniſtra parte della ſtrada, la quale pian piano aſcendendo conduce alla fabrica; fa due peſchiere co i loro beueratori ſopra la ſtrada commune: d'onde partitaſi; adacqua il Bruolo, ilquale è grandiſsimo, e pieno di frutti eccellentiſsimi, e di diuerſe ſeluaticine. La facciata della caſa del padrone hà quattro colonne di ordine Ionico: il capitello di quelle de gli angoli fa fronte da due parti: i quai capitelli come ſi facciano; porrò nel libro de i Tempij. Dall'vna, e l'altra parte ui ſono loggie, le quali nell'eſtremità hanno due colombare, e ſotto quelle ui ſono luoghi da fare i uini, e le ſtalle, e gli altri luoghi per l'vſo di Villa.

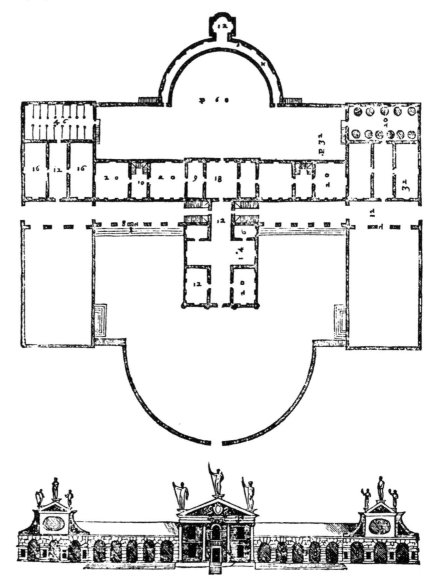

Andrea Palladio. Description, plan, and elevation of villa Barbaro at Maser (I Quattro Libri dell'Architettura, Venice, 1570, Book II, chaper XIV).

a source of inspiration to Palladio when they were working together on that edition of Vitruvius.

The choice of site for the villa (not on the crest of the hill, like a vastle, nor in the middle of a plain like the villas which formed the nucleus of an agricultural activity) is perfect for the Renaissance man, both for the ease of access, and for its distance from the drak woods, the unhealthiness of the swamps and the fogs of the plains. This choice was determined by the earlier presence of the Barbaros in the area, and by the fact that that hill had already been chosen as the ideal site for a home. Maybe in the intervening years they might have built a castle here, or perhaps a religious building with a place to bury their dead. The presence of the spring which gives its name to the locality, and to which Scamozzi refers to as that "beautiful spring of Maser," would seem to suggest that at one time there was a temple here, or at least somewhere where the local people could worship the gods of the place.

It is this same spring which determined the site of the Palladian complex. As with many villas, the spring at Maser constituted the nucleus and the power supply – the Greeks would say *omphalos* – of the habitation. Water, in fact, came to assume a profound significance and was connected with ancient tales, myths, which claimed that the spring was that unique link between this life and the past. When Palladio is discussing Maser on his *Trattato*, he doesn't waste time talking about ideals, values, and the language of art, which he rightly condemns as unworthy of mention, but discusses at greater length than usual the spring, whose water, having supplied the needs of the villa, feeds the fish ponds which are located in front of the southern façade, and also irrigates the gardens and the orchards which extend along the hill.

Villa Barbaro faces south – as do most country houses which do not have to cope with the problems of roads, squares, and neighbors – in obedience to the laws of nature and of astrology, to the benefit of the inhabitants and to the benefit also of the crops stored in the spacious granaries. This "solar" location of Maser is also influenced by the architectural organization of the building which, in order to use the official areas of the villa to the best advantage, interrupts the horizontal development and pushes forward the more decorated central section, as if to present itself to the visitor and welcome the guest. The presence of the semicolumns and the tympanum at the center of the villa accentuate the symmetry of the building, clearly a classical reference, whilst the corner towers of the dovecotes allude to a medieval tradition that had really outlived its function of attracting doves and other fowls to, eventually, the lord's table. The right hand dovecote in fact houses the sun-dial, connecting the villa to the world of the stars, so important to the life of Renaissance man. But let us stop and look at the façade of the villa, so like one of those temples discussed and illustrated by Palladio in one of the chapters of his *Quattro Libri dell'Architettura*. "In all the villas and also in some of the city houses I have put a frontispiece on the forward façade where the principal doors are because such frontispieces accentuate the entrance to the house and add very much to the grandeur and magnificence of the work, being thus made more eminent than the other parts. Besides they prove to be especially useful for the builder's coat of arms, which are usually put on the middle of the façade, as can be seen in the remains of the temples and other public buildings."

The visitor who approaches the balcony of the first floor, turns round and looks towards the interior with his back to the landscape, receives the same impression as he who turns towards the presbytery of a holy building. The most sacred and holy part of the house is the central salon, called the Olympus Salon, whose vaulted ceiling possesses the mystical significance of a dome, and whose decorations, which were entrusted to Paolo Veronese, convey the principal messages of Maser. Beyond the north wall there is a secret internal courtyard where we can find the famous spring. This sacred place is not dedicated to the fortunes of the Barbaro family, but to the local divinities. It is only at this point that the visitor pauses; having

Villa Barbaro seen from the old entrance: in the foreground the fountain of Neptune. In the background, the wooded hill from which rises the "beautiful spring of Masera" which gave its name to the place.

passed through the "nave" and the "presbytery," he has at last reached the shrine of the temple. The water gushes out of the rock and is collected in a circular bowl, which is at the center of a Roman inspired nympheum. Its fame and importance arise more from the secret messages it bears concerning the spring and on the decoration of the grotto, than from the sculpture of the nymphaeum itself, which was probably the work of Daniele Barbaro. Above the nymphaeum Paolo Veronese has portrayed a young queen who, as she is accompanied by a lion, has been interpreted as the allegorical figure of Venice.

The vaulted Salon of Olympus, which we have compared to a profane presbytery, is the urbanistic as well as the spiritual center of the villa. To the right and to the left stretches and enfilade of rooms, anthropomorphically symmetrical like the transepts of a cruciform church.

Up till now we have discussed the ideals, values, and the significance of the heroic glorification at Maser and of the Barbaro family, but this building is also a significant example of those practical aspects which so interested Palladio. As well as being the beloved home of its clients Maser also functioned as what was termed a *villa dell'utile*, or a working farm. The two porticos that flank the central portion as well as being stylistically functional, also serve as agricultural wings, designed to house the farm carts and agricultural implements, to protect the hay from the weather – sheltering it from the sudden storms and from the fierce sun – and, especially, to preserve the precious crops.

Anyone who has visited a Palladian villa and has admired the nobility of the architecture and the wealth of decoration inside is always surprised, if not shocked, to find hardly any information about the said art in the *Quattro Libri*. "The cellars, the granaries, the stables and other outbuildings of this villa," writes Palladio of Villa Emo di Fanzolo, "are at one end and at the other of the main house and at these extremities there are two dovecotes which are useful to the owner and an ornament to the place, and one can go everywhere under cover, which is one of the most desirable things in a villa. Behind this building there is a square garden of eighty Treviso fields, through which runs a river, which makes the site beautiful and agreeable. It has been decorated with painting by Messer Battista Venetiano." That's all, nothing else. He says much the same for Villa Finale and for the other buildings with porticos used for agricultural purposes.

Here is the description of Maser from the *Quattro Libri:* "The building below is at Maser, a Villa near Asolo Castello del Trevigiano, of Monsignor Reverendissimo Eletto di Aquilea and of magnifico Signor Marc'Antonio, the de' Barbari brothers. That part of the building which projects forward, has two levels of rooms. The floor of the upper story is at the same level as the pavement of the courtyard at the rear, where the mountain has been cut away and there is a fountain decorated with infinite amounts of stucco and paint. This spring makes a small lake that serves as a fish pond. From here the water leaves and flows into the kitchen, and then it irrigates the gardens which are to the right and the left of part of the road, which, slowly climbing, leads up to the building. It (the water) then makes two fish ponds with their drinking troughs above the public road, from where it parts, and waters the garden that is very large and full of excellent fruit trees and various bushes. The façade of the house has four columns of the Ionic order; the capitals and the corner ones face in two directions. I found these temples and how they are made from the book on temples. On the one side and on the other there are loggias, whose extremities have dovecotes, and under these there are places to make wine, and the stables, and the other outbuildings for the use of the villa."

Here again we can see that the writer makes absolutely no reference to the sculptors and painters who carried out decorations of the villa. This has suggested the existence of ill-feeling on the part of the architect, especially toward Paolo Veronese, but of this we have no record. James Ackerman is right when he claims that the two artists were in fact made for one another, both inspired by classical ideals, by the arts of ancient

Beyond the slope of the garden stands Villa Barbaro whose central section is flanked by two lateral wings with dovecotes. Yet these elements, typical of villa architecture originally connected to agricultural activities, are here sublimated in a superior and ideal unity which makes this Palladian masterpiece the typical residence of a great humanist to whom the countryside represents not so much profit, but a place to enjoy his literary pursuits.

was a perfect circle with chapels on the four axes. Volumetrically it is a cylinder, surmounted by a hemispherical cupola. The walls have been left bare, there is absolutely no painting, and the decoration is exclusively sculptural. If Alberti had been able to see the Tempietto he would surely have been able to sense the 'Divine Presence'." This building was constructed outside the villa walls on the other side of the public road, so it could be used by the villagers.

With other villas this sort of "proposal" would have instigated the development and would have been the matrix of an inhabited area. However, this was not the case at Maser. The Tempietto still stands alone opposite the villa, for it was the attachment of the Barbaros to the integrity of their home and possessions that defeated any intentions of a social character which Palladio may have had. As the Barbaro and their descendants were able to hold on to the land surrounding the villa, it became a unicum to which no other building was able to aspire: a symbol, perhaps too perfect, for everyday life; an unrepeatable and so particularly fascinating ivory tower.

*Villa Barbaro, details of
the garden populated by
statues of gods and
goddesses.*

Paolo Veronese. Figures looking over the edge of the trompe l'oeil *balcony of the Salon of Olympus.*

From the trompe l'oeil *door a gentleman comes in from the hunt with his dogs.*

Paolo Veronese.
(1528–1588)

One of the most famous Venetian painters of the Renaissance, Paolo Veronese has left many examples of his genius, especially in the frescos of the Venetian villas, thus creating a genre which his followers and disciples admired and imitated. Paolo Caliari was born in Verona in 1528; at the age of 20 he painted his first documented work, followed by the decorations of Villa Soranza, near Castelfranco. After arriving in Venice around 1553, he achieved great fame with the canvases destined for the ceilings of Ducal Palace, and with his decorations for the church of San Sebastiano. Apart from his large canvases portraying "The Wedding-Feast of Cana," "The Banquet of Gregory the Great," "The Guests in the House of Levi," his portraits and allegorical and mythological paintings are also very well known. From time to time he worked as a fresco-painter and decorator in the Venetian palaces and villas. Circa 1560 he executed one of the most significant cycle of paintings in the Veneto, by frescoing the rooms of Villa Barbaro at Maser, which proved a source of inspiration for most of the artists working in the Venetian villas in the second half of the Cinquecento. Paolo died in Venice in 1588.

Villa Barbaro, Salon of Olympus; in the vaulted ceiling the heavenly gods with the signs of the Zodiac; in the center the allegory of Divine Wisdom with a serpent symbolizing Eternity; in the lunette are portrayed "Summer" and "Autumn." In the detail, a young boy holding a book looks over the trompe l'oeil *balustrade.*

Villa Barbaro, Salon of Olympus; between the Corinthian columns are frescoed landscapes with mountains and rivers. The modern furniture was sober.

Salon of Bacchus, fireplace by Alessandro Vittoria with a classical inscription invoking serenity: Ignem in sinu ne abscondas. *In the center of the side wall is a fresco depicting a villa and its avenue with carriages and horsemen.*

172

Andrea Palladio:
*Description, plan, and
elevation of Villa Emo at
Fanzolo* (I Quattro Libri
dell'Architettura, *Venice,
1570, Book II, chapter
XIV*).

SECONDO.   55

A FANZOLO Villa del Triuigiano difcofto da Caftelfranco tre miglia, è la fottopofta fabrica del Magnifico Signor Leonardo Emo. Le Cantine, i Granari, le Stalle, e gli altri luoghi di Villa fono dall'vna, e l'altra parte della cafa dominicale, e nell'eftremità loro vi fono due colombare, che
apportano utile al padrone, & ornamento al luogo, e per tutto fi può andare al coperto: ilche è vna
delle principal cofe, che fi ricercano ad vna cafa di Villa, come è ftato auertito di fopra. Dietro a
quefta fabrica è vn giardino quadro di ottanta campi Triuigiani: per mezo il quale corre vn fiumicel
lo, che rende il fito molto bello, e dilettevole. E' ftata ornata di pitture da M. Battifta Venetiano.

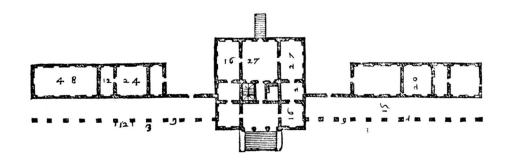

DE I

Villa Emo
Fanzolo di Vedelago, Treviso

The villa of the "magnifico signor Leonardo Emo" at Fanzolo is perhaps the building that corresponds with the greatest clearness to those ideals of concreteness and functionality characteristic of Palladian planning. "The cellars, the granaries, the stables, and the other places of the villa" – writes the Vicentine architect in his *Quattro Libri* – are on each side of the main house, and at their extremities are two dovecotes which are useful for the owner and ornament the place, and everywhere one can go under cover, which is one of the principal things looked for in a villa."

The building, which develops horizontally, almost stretching itself out over the large plain, is flanked by two dovecotes that, however, are not just simple utilitarian buildings but romantic allusions to ancient medieval towers.

This Palladian villa was constructed on the enormous property which Leonardo di Giovanni Emo bought from the Barbarigo family after the battle of Cambrai, in 1509, and which was later inherited by his descendant Leonardo di Alvise. In 1535 or 1536 the Emos were able to buy a stretch of water, the Barbarigo "seriola," a sort of tributary of the Brentella Canal, and they then started work on the reclamation and drainage of their territory, maybe

on the advice of Alvise Cornaro. This perhaps paved the way for the construction of the villa by his successors, the heirs of "that generation of fathers" inspired and guided by Cornaro, and faithful to the ideals of "blessed architecture."

In fact it was precisely in that period that the Emos, being able to utilize the abundant supplies of water, introduced the cultivation of maize, a cereal much richer than the sorghum which had formed the basic food of the peasants up till then.

Architectonically the villa of Fanzolo appears similar to that of Maser, with that arrayment of porticos which creates a perfect fusion between the main building and the agricultural parts. Built between the years 1554 and 1565, with a precision of measurement rare in the Renaissance period, the villa was used for the Emo-Grimani wedding celebrations and probably completed especially for this occasion.

The highest motives that inspired the building of villas in the Cinquecento seem to co-exist in complete harmony at Fanzolo; on the one hand the main residence possesses a tremendous dignity that is not excessive or exaggerated but still maintains a certain aristocratic sobriety, whilst on the other hand the *barchesse* and the other outbuild-

In this building the two components which characterize Palladio's villas – the traditional Venetian barchesse with their dovecotes, and the culture of Rome, clearly seen in the main building, are combined by his ingenious feeling for light and landscape.

Detail of the portico, with
the dovecote.
The central body of the
villa falls into line with
the straight side wings, in
harmony with the
surrounding flat
countryside.

ings in no way detract from the nobility of the central portion. When talking about this villa and Villa Barbaro at Maser, where Palladio "transformed the *barchesse* into loggias on the two sides of a temple," Ackerman notes the "various messages" transmitted by the architect "on the theme of the villa:" "While his geometric axial forms make a subtle contrast to the organic world, the total composition extends out to embrace the surrounding area, while its cupolas and the sacred pediment of its façade possess their own sense of urbanity and communicate, and thus at the same time celebrate, the social status of the family by means of classical know-how and religious tradition. Palladio often unites some elements from a normal agricultural farm to these characteristics."

Inside the villa, Zelotti's paintings correspond perfectly to the ideals that guided the inhabitants of the villa: the scenes and people portrayed allude, in fact, to those historic or mythological episodes that constituted an irreplaceable fundamental ethic of the culture of the Venetian villas.

179

Eulogy to the agrarian life

The dualism between the city and the country, theorized since the times of ancient Rome, seemed to have deeply interested the humanists of the Quattrocento and Cincequento. Petrarch had already recounted the advantages of living in the country as opposed to life in the bustling, frenetic city. In the country passions are exalted, man finds redemption from the negative influence of the city, and virtue triumphs. In fact it is virtue which distinguishes a gentleman, which raises him up and confers prestige upon him; it is not by accident that in the frescos of the villas one often finds tribute to the virtuous behaviour of the great men of the past, such as Alexander the Great and Scipio.

In the isolation of the country and the agrarian world, passions are overcome and vices are defeated: the villa becomes a place of virtue that influences those who are fortunate enough to live under its roof, offering the choice of peace and tranquility, study, or industry, from which wealth is derived. This seems to be the scheme of things, which, prompted by the Emos, form the message of Zelotti's frescos.

In the main salon examples of the Virtue and Chastity of the ancients are recalled by the "Episodes of Scipio," while in the hall one is reminded that through "Prudence" one obtains "Abundance" and "Wealth."

In the Salon of the Arts one is encouraged to cultivate the studies of Astronomy, Poetry, Music, Sculpture, Architecture, and Painting. Above the fireplace are references to the Seasons that regulate all the activities of the countryside. In the other rooms characters and scenes from mythology give the artist ample opportunity to demonstrate his skill at landscapes and pastoral scenes.

Giambattista Zelotti.
Detail from a painted
decoration with a
grotesque and the Emo
family's coat of arms.

Giambattista Zelotti.
Doorway with the
allegorical figures of
Prudence and Abundance,
the vaulted ceiling of the
vestibule is decorated with
a pergola of vines.

Salon of Venus, above the
fireplace a fresco by
Giambattista Zelotti
showing Venus wounded
by love.

*Giambattista Zelotti.
Detail from a painted
decoration with a
grotesque and the Emo
family's coat of arms.*

*Giambattista Zelotti.
Doorway with the
allegorical figures of
Prudence and Abundance,
the vaulted ceiling of the
vestibule is decorated with
a pergola of vines.*

*Salon of Venus, above the
fireplace a fresco by
Giambattista Zelotti
showing Venus wounded
by love.*

184

*Villa Emo, the Salon of
Venus, frescos by
Giambattista Zelotti, with
the scene showing a goddess
helping the wounded
Adonis.*

Giambattista Zelotti.
Venus tries to prevent
Adonis from taking part
in the hunt.

*Giambattista Zelotti.
Detail from a painted
decoration with a
grotesque and the Emo
family's coat of arms.*

*Giambattista Zelotti.
Doorway with the
allegorical figures of
Prudence and Abundance,
the vaulted ceiling of the
vestibule is decorated with
a pergola of vines.*

*Salon of Venus, above the
fireplace a fresco by
Giambattista Zelotti
showing Venus wounded
by love.*

Villa Foscari
known as "La Malcontenta"
Mira, Venice

Not far from Venice, on the banks of the Brenta, stands the magnificent Palladian Villa Foscari, perhaps better known as "the Malcontenta;" the first of a series of villas that flowered in the terra firma during the rule of the Serenissima. Today that green plain, salvaged centuries ago from the mosquito-ridden swamps by Venetian landowners, is again in danger, this time not from floods but from continuous encroachment by the industries of Marghera, whose fumes suffocate and corrode the very fabric of the villas.

When Albert Landsberg bought the villa, it was being used for the cultivation of silk worms, which he promptly stopped in time to save some of the frescos. Fortunately times have changed and today there are a sufficient number of people who are aware of the immense historical and artistic value of our enormous architectural patrimony.

Without doubt one of the most fascinating of all Palladian buildings, la Malcontenta is reflected in the waters of the Brenta, which give it life and make it even more beautiful. Rivers were very important indeed in the past as they were a very popular and economic means of communication. "If one can build on a river," writes Palladio, "it will be very convenient and beautiful since one can always reach the city with little expense..., and the view is very beautiful, and very easily and with great ornament one can water the possessions, the gardens, and the kitchen gardens, which are the life and recreation of the villa."

Palladio solved the problem of high water and flooding by placing the piano nobile on a base which both enhances the majesty of the building and lets it be seen from afar. "This building is raised eleven feet above the ground," Palladio, in fact, writes.

The Brenta, so important in the history of the villa, also determined its siting, thus changing the usual building typology, for the principle façade faces north to overlook the river, presenting the dignity and solemnity of its Ionic loggia to its guests and travellers passing by. On the south side however, Palladio breaks up the massive block of the buildings with different shaped openings which let the early afternoon light inundate the lofty interior.

The typical sobriety of Palladian masterpieces is at last encountered in the sides of the building; the extremely sparing distribution of cornices and openings and the graduated use of ashlar-work contribute much to the beauty and harmony of the whole complex.

The villa is richly decorated with frescos: Battista Franco started those in the Salon of the Giants, which remind one of the Mantuan paintings of Giulio Romano, and they were completed by Giambattista Zelotti, painter of the grotesques and landscapes that can be reconstructed or at least visualized from the descriptions of Ridolfi. Mythological scenes alternate with Allegories of the Arts and of Virtue, with the usual references to villa life symbolised by "Astraea showing Jove the pleasures of the Earth."

Built around 1560 and within easy reach of the city, the villa was mainly used for official receptions, such as that given for Henry III in 1574.

Andrea Palladio.
Description, plan and
elevation of Villa Foscari
(I Quattro Libri
dell'Architettura, *Venice*
1570, Book II, chapter
XIV).

NON MOLTO lungi dalle Gambarare fopra la Brenta è la feguente fabrica delli Magnifici
Signori Nicolò, e Luigi de' Foſcari.   Queſta fabrica è alzata da terra undici piedi, e ſotto ui ſono cu
cine, tinelli, e ſimili luoghi, & è fatta in uolto coſì di ſopra, come di ſotto.   Le ſtanze maggiori hanno i
uolti alti ſecondo il primo modo delle altezze de' uolti. Le quadre hanno i uolti à cupola: ſopra i ca
merini vi ſono mezati: il uolto della Sala è à Crociera di mezo cerchio: la ſua impoſta è tanto alta dal
piano, quanto è larga la Sala: la quale è ſtata ornata di eccellentiſsime pitture da Meſſer Battiſta Venetiano.   Meſſer Battiſta Franco grandiſsimo diſegnatore à noſtri tempi hauea ancor eſſo dato prin
cipio à dipingere una delle ſtanze grandi, ma ſoprauenuto dalla morte ha laſciata l'opera imperfetta.
La loggia è di ordine Ionico: La Cornice gira intorno tutta la caſa, e fa fronteſpicio ſopra la loggia, e
nella parte oppoſta.   Sotto la Gronda vi è vn'altra Cornice, che camina ſopra i frontespicij: Le ca-
mere di ſopra ſono come mezati per la loro baſſezza, perche ſono alte ſolo otto piedi.

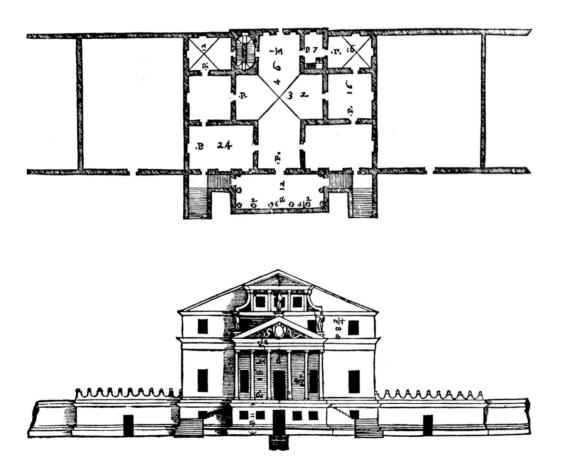

LA SOTTOPOSTA

"I would liken the salon, loggia and garden where you live to a bride who waits for her new kinsfolk to come and welcome her."
(Pietro Aretino, Lettere, *1609).*

Palladio's beautiful and noble architecture seems to welcome the travelers who come down the busy Brenta. Even today Villa Malcontenta is like a Roman dream come true, overlooking the waters of the canal, which, as more and more patrician residences were built along its banks, became a sort of Grand Canal for those who fled from Venice for their villeggiatura.

189

Villa Caldogno

Caldogno, Vicenza

*Despite the absence of
precise documentation
regarding the authorship of
this building, the
compositional rhythms that
echo other documented
works by Palladio - such
as the relief of the three
ashlar-work arches on
the otherwise plain
wall, the tympanum, the
original polygonal
steps – are all elements
which suggest that this
is another example of
Palladio's work.*

In about 1565, Angelo Caldogno, a Vicentine aristocrat and friend of Andrea Palladio, commissioned the architect to build a villa to the north of Vicenza in the heart of an area long dominated by the presence of his family. Even though it does not appear among the pages of the *Quattro Libri*, its solid architectonic structure and the simplicity of its exterior, elegant in its purity, suggest the hand of Andrea. This is so much so, that it does not seem wise to attribute this house to Piero di Nanto as has been done by several historians. Its Palladian paternity would seem not only to be confirmed by the friendship that existed between the architect and the noble Vicentine, but, apart from this historical fact, also by the undeniable artistic quality of this villa and its affinity with other documented creations of Palladio.

The principal prospect of the house is particularly significant with its three great arches strongly outlined by the ashlar-work cornice that spans the portico, its only decorative element. Furthermore, the simplicity and bareness that characterise the surface of the walls suggest an ideal parallel to Palladio's early works, particularly that of Villa Saraceno at Finale.

The interior decorations are especially beautiful and were for the most part executed by Giovanni Antonio Fasolo, who, in the loggia and main salon, illustrates the amusements and pleasures of life in the villa. The frescos of the loggia are dedicated to depicting those very pleasant days spent playing cards and listening to concerts, or indeed dancing and banqueting.

Zelotti also worked at Villa Caldogno where he painted "The History of Scipio and Sophonisba," whilst later on, with the portrayal of Pastor Fido, Carpioni would introduce a motif dealing with a literary theme.

Of particular interest are some figures with carefully painted physiognomy. These are probably portraits of the more important members of the Caldogno family.

The interior of the villa is
enlivened by rich frescos,
which illustrate the
amusements and delights of
villa life.

Giovanni Antonio Fasolo;
Frescos in the main salon
with scenes from "The
Dance" and "The Card
Game."

On the following pages:
details from "The Dance,"
"The Concerto," and "The
Card Game."

Villa Cornaro

Piombino Dese, Padua

The villa that Palladio designed, in about 1553, for the Venetian nobleman Giorgio Cornaro, has had a difficult and tormented history. In his will, dated 1570, Cornaro requests that a certain sum of money should be put aside "as long as the construction of the palace continue": a significant codicil that lets us understand that once the building of the villa had begun, his heirs had to respect the wishes of their predecessor and finish it. This codicil is also an example of the importance of the concept of continuity to the Venetians. This was a concept particularly praised by all those who were involved with the history of the Venetian villas, from Alvise Cornaro to Palladio himself.

Still unfinished in 1582, the villa was enhanced with an upper loggia in 1596, and only in a drawing dated 1613 do we see it in its final form. Probably the superimposition of constructive phases and the series of modifications can explain the weakness of the architecture, scarcely homogeneous and devoid of any truly harmonious agreement between its various parts.

Built more as a suburban residence than a working "villa-farm," it is characterized by the presence of two *piani nobili*, one on top of the other, an unusual occurrence for a country villa but often found in the city.

The villa stands close to a river and possesses a garden with flower beds as well as fish ponds. The principal prospect, divided up by columns that are too slender and marked by a too scarce agreement between the floors, looks out onto the road. In fact, it almost seems part of it, as is the case with many Settecento villas. Flanked by other dwellings, the Cornaro residence somehow contradicts the usual "princely autonomy" of the other Palladian villas.

In the interior there are portraits of the Cornaro family attributed to Camillo Mariani; an example of self-celebration, which is an exception to the usual iconography.

Alongside the main house are the usual agricultural buildings that at one time, as can be seen in an eighteenth-century drawing, were dominated by a dovecote.

A classic example of "open architecture," characterized by porticos and loggias, the Cornaro's villa has become, despite its evident stylistic incongruities, one of the most widely imitated models of English and American Palladianism.

Facing the public road, this villa, whose double order of columns confers on it the dignity of a palace, is one of the most imitated models of English and American Palladianism.

198

*Andrea Palladio.
Description, plan, and
elevation of Villa Cornaro
at Piombino Dese
(I Quattro Libri
dell'Architettura,
Venice 1570, book II,
chapter XIV).*

LA FABRICA, che fegue è del Magnifico Signor Giorgio Cornaro in Piombino luogo di Caftel Franco. Il primo ordine delle loggie è Ionico.   La Sala è pofta nella parte più a dentro della cafa, accioche fia lontana dal caldo, e dal freddo : le ale oue fi ueggono i nicchi fono larghe la terza parte della fua lunghezza : le colonne rifpondono al diritto delle penultime delle loggie , e fono tanto diftanti tra fe, quanto alte : le ftanze maggiori fono lunghe un quadro, e tre quarti : i uolti fono alti fecondo il primo modo delle altezze de' volti : le mediocri fono quadre il terzo più alte che larghe ; i uolti fono à lunette : fopra i camerini vi fono mezati. Le loggie di fopra fono di ordine Corinthio : le colonne fono la quinta parte più fottili di quelle di fotto. Le ftanze fono in folaro,& hanno fopra alcuni mezati. Da vna parte ui è la cucina , e luoghi per maffare , e dall'altra i luoghi per feruitori.

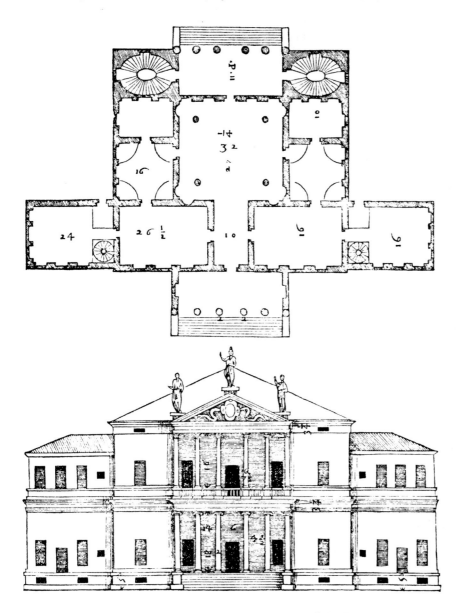

LA SOTTOPOSTA

*Villa Cornaro, as seen
from the garden.*

*Salon of the four columns,
detail: in the niche is a
plaster statue of a member
of the Cornaro family by
Camilo Mariani.*

Villa Almerico Capra
known as "La Rotonda"
Vicenza

This is the most famous and well known of all Palladian villas, considered by the architect as a city residence because it was built on the immediate outskirts of Vicenza and was devoid of all agricultural functions.

The acropolic position, crowning a small hill, makes it a stunning belvedere that looks out, thanks to its four equal prospects, over all the surrounding landscape and admirably realizes the Palladian ideal of "see and be seen."

The client, Paolo Almerico, was a man of the church, being Apostolic Referendary to Popes Pius IV and Pius V. He had lived in Rome and wished to realize his dreams of ambition – his desire to win the respect and admiration of his fellow citizens. Ackerman must have had La Rotonda in mind when he wrote: "The mythical dimension of the ideology of the villa frees it from the concrete limitations of a utilitarian and productive nature and makes it the perfect place to demonstrate the creative aspirations of both the client and the architect."

Inspired by the most noble examples of Rome and crowned by a dome, like a sacred temple, the villa still manages to possess a completely Venetian character, due to its cordial relationship with the surrounding landscape. It, therefore, appears as a living and vibrant presence, with none of the coldness and rigidity of an exclusively architectural taste.

In fact, the Rotonda was designed to appear as the top of the hill upon which it was built: the steps follow the natural slope of the hill and the dome crowns the villa just as the villa crowns the hill. Thus the classical elements became almost an emanation of the landscape; the pronaos surmounted by a tympanum is no longer the vertex of a hierarchy, as it is repeated on all four sides, letting the visitor enjoy the countryside from every point of view. The culmination of the villa is thus the dome, which Palladio had studied at Rome, particularly in his idealized reconstruction of the Baths of Caracalla, as a dominant element also in profane buildings.

Often referred to as Villa Capra, it actually is an expression of the culture of Paolo Almerico, who

The villa was conceived by Palladio as a monument to the client: Paolo Almerico from Vicenza, Apostolic Referendary of Popes Pius IV and Pius V. Built on top of a hill, this villa, crowned by a dome like a Greek temple, is characterized above all by the motif of the Ionic pronaos, or portico, which is repeated on all four sides, almost as if to underline its celebratory character.

already possessed a princely palace in the city, but wanted to build a monument to his personality in this charming countryside. Such a desire is only comprehensible when seen against the background of a particular climate that was widespread in the sixteenth century, and that had more or less affected all of Palladio's clients.

Almerico's desire to perpetuate the glory of his *gens* was but a short-lived dream, his son sold the villa to the Capra family, the ideals changed rapidly, and the inscription put up by the new proprietors deprived the Rotonda of its idealized function as a lay and profane monument, placing it firmly instead in the category of traditional country villas. The Capra, who had bought up all the surrounding land, had more concern for their new union with the country than of the glory of their family.

MEMORIAE PERPETVAE MANDANS
HAEC DVM SVSTINET AC
ABSTINET

La Rotonda, the central salon with frescos by Ludovico Dorigny and by an unknown quadraturista *who multiplies illusionistically the architectonic effects of the building.*

Villa Serego

Santa Sofia di San Pietro in Cariano,
Verona

Santa Sofia di San Pietro in Caraino takes its name
from the ancient church of Santa Sofia, already
annexed to a previous villa that Antonio Della
Scala had given to the *condottiere*, Cortesia Serego.
The documents that supply this information also
mention a high dovecote, a cistern, a wine press,
and other agricultural equipment.

Saving the church, Palladio started construction
of the present villa sometime between 1560 and
1570, probably the project had a long gestation
period (some say it started as early as 1551).

The building complex is surrounded by a large
park, and the whole is outstandingly beautiful,
as Palladio himself notes in the *Quattro Libri*:
"Situated in a wonderful position, that is on top
of a hill that is very easily climbed and it looks out
over part of the city and it is between two small
valleys; all the hills around are very pleasant
and full of very good water, so therefore this
building is adorned with gardens and marvellous
fountains..."

The villa is a rather unusual example of Palladio's
work, who was always as receptive to the various
exigencies and aspirations of his clients as he was to
the varying landscapes in which he worked. In this
particular villa he managed to express the military
character of this Veronese family, erecting an edifice
that, had it been completed according to his plans,
would have resulted in a massive architectural
complex, complete with three courtyards nestling in
the hilly surroundings.

The only part of the project that was actually built
brings us back to one of those three principles that
inspired Palladio's work: durability. Time, in fact,
has hardly had an effect on the plaster, and the
rudely cut rocks piled up one on top of another,
which form the columns, are almost harsh and
primitive in their massive solidarity. The plastic
density of the ashlar-work on these columns, which
are all of the same order, expresses a grandeur and
strength equalled only by Michelangelo. Palladio
was obviously thinking of these "stones not
cleaned" when he wrote that "the villa needs
elements that are straightforward and simple rather
than delicate."

*Adapting himself to the
military traditions of the
Veronese aristocracy and
interpreting the Serego's
aspirations to power,
Palladio conceived this
villa using the intensely
expressive strength of the
materials and the
buildings, which recall his
experiences of the
architecture of ancient
Rome and the mannerism
of Giulio Romano.*

214

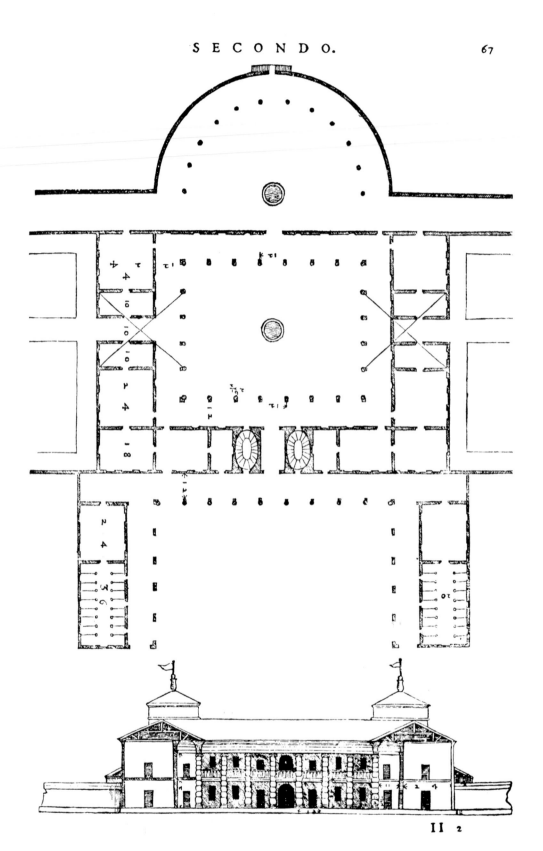

Andrea Palladio. Plan, and description of Villa Serego at Santa Sofia (I Quattro Libri dell'Architettura, *Venice, 1570, book II, chapter XV*).

More than anything designed by Sanmicheli or Giulio Romano, Villa Serego makes us think immediately of the buildings of ancient Rome.

Inside the old chapel of Santa Sofia there are frescos dating from the Trecento.

The presence of Romans in this area, also mentioned by Palladio apropos this villa, is revived in the powerful form of this architecture.

Villa Serego, the "stones not cleaned" underline the sheer weight of the material, in contrast with the more well-known forms of Palladio.

Villa Campiglia Negri de' Salvi

Albettone, Vicenza

The spread of Romanticism in the nineteenth century brought about much rebuilding, and sometimes even demolition, of the old villas, carried out on the orders of owners who felt that their homes had become inadequate and no longer fulfilled the needs of those modern, different times.

The most famous protagonist of such "tampering" in the Vicenza area was a certain architect called Antonio Caregaro Negrin, who in 1842 was commissioned by the Negri de' Salvi to "gothicize" their residence at Albettone. Fortunately one ground floor room of this Quattrocento building, which had belonged to the noble Campiglia family, was saved. This had been frescoed by Giovanni Antonio Fasolo between the years 1560 and 1570 with scenes depicting various aspects of life in a villa and which were especially interesting and delightful because of the elegance of the figures and the naturalness of their poses.

The frescos portraying "Music," "Games," and "the Chase" were heavily repainted by Giovanni Busato in 1858. Only recently have careful restorations returned them to their original charm and vivacity.

In their fascinating entirety, the cycle of frescos at Albettone provide us with the most complete image of what life was like in the villa of an aristocratic Venetian, a style of life that lasted throughout the whole of the Settecento. Alongside the equestrian pursuit of hunting and the games that helped pass the time in the villa, music represents the call of the arts.

Many of these villas acted as true academies, as was noted by Palladio himself when describing Villa Repeta in Campiglia, not far from Albettone.

From the ancient dwelling of the Campiglia, restored in the Ottocento, was saved one room in which Giovanni Antonio Fasolo had painted various episodes and amusements from villa life.

Giovanni Antonio Fasolo; detail from "The Concert."

On the following pages: "The game of Tric-Trac" and "Three gentlemen playing flutes."

Villa Obizzi
called "Il Catajo"
Battaglia, Padua

Erected around 1570, this castle-villa, symbol of the endurance of chivalrous sentiment over the centuries, faithfully mirrors the military ideal of the man who commissioned it, Pio Enea degli Obizzi, condottiere in the service of the Serene Republic.

Evoking remote legends, the Catajo castle, which rises up at the foot of the Euganean Hills near Monselice, constitutes one of the most extraordinary architectural complexes of the Venetian mainland. Erected around 1570 by the *condottiere* of the Venetian Republic, Pio Enea degli Obizzi, whose name derives from the invention of a kind of firearm (the *obice*, or howitzer), the castle clearly reflects the military ideals of the man who had it built. The crenellated turrets, triumphal arches, drawbridge, and the massive, austere structure of the central part eloquently allude to the art of war to which Enea degli Obizzi and his guests devoted their lives. Nevertheless, the present-day structure of the building does not fully correspond to the original design, which tradition maintains was drafted by Obizzi himself.

For the fresco decorations – even the façade was painted, as one can see in the print by Volkamer – Obizzi turned to Giambattista Zelotti and to other artists who, in the various rooms, retold episodes from Roman history and more recent war scenes in which the Obizzis had figured prominently. Now deprived of the decorative finishings which once softened its forms, the façade presents itself in all its massive severity. New architectural complexes were later added to the original main block, and it became necessary to flatten further the surrounding hills to facilitate transportation to nearby centers.

The Courtyard of the Giants, constructed in the seventeenth century, was the site of numerous jousts, while the theater housed spectacles and dramas. The work of expansion was carried on by subsequent owners, members of noble families who enriched the castle with whimsical structures and displays, such as the nineteenth-century decoration of the chapel in German Gothic style.

The Catajo stands as a testimony of the endurance of chivalric nostalgia over the centuries. The castle gained particular prestige when works of art, antiques, and precious musical instruments were collected and shown in its rooms; unfortunately, however, these collections were broken up at the end of the last century and are now scattered in various foreign museums.

Villa Eolia

Costozza di Longare, Vicenza

Among those villas whose proprietors included Renaissance humanists, we find the wonderful Villa Eolia, or "Prison of the Winds," at Costozza. It was built, according to Renaissance architect Andrea Palladio, by the remarkable gentleman Francesco Trento. By using a network of wind ducts, he took advantage of the intermittenly cool and warm air of the caves and galleries of the nearby Berici hills to make more pleasurable the scholarly gatherings held there, which brought together some of the most celebrated figures of the time. Palladio writes: "... as there are in the same hills as the said Villa a number of very large caves… in which some very fresh winds originate, these Gentlemen, by means of underground passageways that they call wind ducts, convey [these winds] to their houses, and with pipes similar to these ducts they convey the cool wind to all of their rooms, closing them and opening them as they please to obtain more or less coolness, depending on the season" (from *The Four Books of Architecture*, 1570).

The scholars gathered at Villa Eolia thus could always enjoy a mild atmosphere, thanks to the air coming up from the cryptoporticus below and flowing into the house through a grating in the floor. Originally the name Eolia belonged to the underground hollow, and on its entrance door one can still be read today: AEOLUS HIC CLAUSO VENTORUM CARCERE REGNAT AEOLIA.

Outside, the building has an extremely simple, unadorned surface, in marked contrast with the decorative richness of the interior. Divided by painted, illusory architectural elements, the walls contain vast landscapes, while above, in the cross-vault, is a sky peopled with deities according to the seasons and the Zodiac. The entire decorative display seems to converge toward the center of the dome where, enclosed in an octagon, the radiant image of Apollo-Helios hovers, symbol of the neo-Platonic culture that inspired the iconography of the room. These frescos, evidently inspired by Veronese, are the work of various painters, though mostly of Giovanni Antonio Fasolo, one of the most famous fresco painters of the Vicenza region.

Of particular significance is the cryptoporticus – also painted in fresco by Fasolo – which seems to express the will to establish a new, almost osmotic relationship with the underground realm. Overturning the motif that inspired Rotonda, whose architecture crowns the countryside, Villa Eolia seems ideally to embrace and dominate the more mysterious and recondite forces of nature.

The ceiling of the hall of Villa Eolia, with frescos attributed to Giovanni Antonio Fasolo. In the middle is Aeolus, in the niches the allegories of the Four Seasons flanked by Olympian deities on chariots drawn by animals sacred to them.

Two details portraying Mars and Venus.

Villa Barbarigo
Noventa Vicentina, Vicenza

The villa that the dogal Barbarigo family built at Noventa Vicentina in the late 1500s stands as one of the most emblematic expressions of the "villa culture" that for centuries characterized the Venetian countryside. Indeed, this villa embodies the deepest significance and the noblest purpose of the patrician villas on the mainland, which were seen as symbols of the Venetian aristocracy and destined to become cornerstones of the surrounding territory. If over the course of time much of the villa's original significance has been lost, its role as the pulsating heart of local life remains nevertheless alive and tangible. What is most striking even today is how the town of Noventa developed and organized itself around this exceptionally unified architectural complex. In particular, there are the two wings of annexes cadenced by Tuscan columns, which enclose a large grain market-square, a reminder of the once-thriving farming industry, now transformed by the monument to the war dead which rises up at its center.

Two very clear and precise intentions seem to have guided the Barbarigos in this undertaking: the quest for revenue – their land holdings were vast in the region – and the desire for political affirmation. Both intentions are represented in the frescos adorning the villa, and next to scenes of battle and scenes exalting the glory of the *gens*, we find mythological representations celebrating deities connected to agriculture. The subjects of these paintings, attributed for the most part to Antonio Foler and Antonio Vassilacchi (called "l'Aliense"), have led us to call the Noventa villa the "Villa of the Doges," a title which Loukomski erroneously gave to all the villas of the region. Aside from the portraits of the Doges Marco and Agostino Barbarigo, there are representations of other members of the dogal house in various other rooms, next to celebrations of their deeds in peace and in war, performed in the name of Venice and St. Mark.

While the decorations on the top floor are devoted to the celebration of culture and the arts, especially those done by Luca Ferrari da Reggio, the frescos on the first floor have a primarily

The title of "Villas of the Doges" that Loukomski gave to the villas of Venetia is particularly applicable to Villa Barbarigo at Noventa, especially because of its portraits of the Barbarigo doges and its cycle of frescos depicting the wartime and peacetime deeds of this family.

RESIDENZA MUNICIPALE

"political" function. In the *Hall with the Portrait of the Doge Marco*, we see the meaningful allegories of *Peace triumphing over destroyed arms*, *Wisdom*, and *Obedience* – virtues which lead to *Fame*. In the *Hall with the Portrait of the Doge Agostino*, on the other hand, we find allegories of *Beauty*, *Love*, *Fame*, *Fortune*, and *War*.

As with the building's architecture – solemn and majestic with the colonnades that distinguish both the main body and the annexes – what matters most in the paintings is the display of political prestige by these "talking walls," which are like an open book on the glories of the Barbarigo family.

As Andrea Palladio said in his *Four Books of Architecture* (1570), "… the Architect should realize above all that great Gentlemen, especially those of the Republic, require houses with loggias and spacious, ornate rooms, so that in these places they can entertain those who are waiting to greet the patron, or to ask him for help, or for favors."

Portrait of the doge Agostino Barbarigo, by Antonio Vassiliacchi, known as Aliense.

A Barbarigo ambassador being received by a King. Fresco by Aliense in the Hall of the Ambassadors in Villa Barbarigo.

Villa Contarini

Piazzola sul Brenta, Padua

The history of the villa of Piazzola, which was formerly a fief of the Carraresi and assigned to the noble Contarini family in 1413 after the Venetian expansion onto the mainland, is complex and full of significance. In order to increase their own prestige and jurisdiction over the area, the Contarini built a magnificent villa, which was transformed several times over the centuries. A park approximately 272 acres (110 hectares large) surrounds the palatial villa, around which the entire town of Piazzola grew up and expanded.

The more recent history of the complex starts in 1546, when the central body was erected according to the prototype of the Venetian *palazzo*. To the Cinquecento plan, developed around the central salon famous for its balls and receptions, were added, over the course of the 1600s, the vast wings and their plethora of statues and decoration, evidence of a decadent exaggeration of Baroque art.

Also from the seventeenth century are the interior frescos, which are of considerable interest; those in the *Hall of the Arts and Sciences* are attributed to Dorigny, while those in the *Hall of the Bacchanals* show the strong influence of Giulio

Romano's frescos in the Tea Palace. The *Hall of the Rape of Persephone* is from 1684.

The villa, with its exceptional size, conforms perfectly to the general mood of exaltation and the taste for the spectacular and grandiose, typical of the 1600s and inspired by the great courts of Europe.

The happiest moment in the history of the villa at Piazzola came in 1685, on the occasion of the reception in honor of the Duke of Brunswick, when the fish-pools flanking the building were used for mock naval battles, while in the piazzas triumphal chariots paraded by and masked characters amused the guests.

But art continued to flourish at Piazzola even in later centuries; in 1770 Temanza built the family chapel in the neoclassical style, while the palace's interior was being embellished with new frescos and a collection of important art. The instrumental and choral concerts also gained notoriety, and the Contarini family's commitment to culture extended even to the point of printing editions of considerable importance. In more recent times the villa has taken on a symbolic value. At the

Aerial view of Villa Contarini, and in front, the hemicycle of annexes which describe a large piazza.

The villa's façade and the arches that pass over the fish pond.

beginning of this century one of its last proprietors, acknowledging the transformations taking place in the socioeconomic realm, decided to adapt the palatial complex to productive activities in step with the industrial age. With an enlightened spirit he equipped the place for mechanized farming activities and added lodgings to receive the numerous peasant workers, thus managing to create a self-sufficient farming community, which, in addition, was connected to Padua with a special railway line.

Villa Contarini, one of the rooms with exquisite stuccowork decorations.

Villa Duodo

Monselice, Padua

At Monselice, in the heart of the Euganean hills, there once stood a small fortress of the Carraresi which Venice acquired during its expansion onto the mainland. Its defensive function now obsolete, the castle was given over to three important Venetian families, the most distinguished of which was the Duodo family, "the richest in possessions in Monselice."

At around the close of the sixteenth century Vincento Scamozzi was commissioned by Francesco Duodo to erect, on the site of the old Carrarese stronghold, a villa commensurate with the glory and prestige of his powerful family. The choice of architect was not a casual one; Scamozzi and his patron were on very familiar terms, Duodo having once brought the architect along with him to Poland on an official visit.

In addition, Scamozzi's customary attention to the importance of the landscape and to environmental circumstances gave him the inspired idea of realizing a "Via Sacra" (Holy Way) – a dramatic route from the center of Monselice leading right up to the villa. Along this road, amid the cypresses, seven chapels were erected, enabling the faithful to enjoy the same indulgences that they enjoyed when visiting the seven Basilicas of Rome. The Duodos gave special attention to the little adjoining church that was dedicated to Saint George, which they enriched and embellished with numerous relics that had been given to them by various Popes and put on display for the people's veneration.

Over the centuries modifications were made to the villa with the intention of improving as well as expanding the original structure of the stately complex; a particularly admirable addition was the staircase that was built at the back of the villa, following the slope of the hill.

In 1740 Andrea Tirali built a new wing, also using Euganean trachyte so as not to upset the unity of the construction. In addition, inside the villa there was a wealth of art that included several portraits of illustrious members of the family. The portraits of Pietro and Domenico Duodo, executed by Vittoria, are now kept at the Ca' d'Oro.

The monumental complex of Villa Duodo, with architectures by Vincenzo Scamozzi and Andrea Tirali, the little church of San Giorgio, and the eighteenth-century staircase that follows the slope of the hill.

The end part of the
staircase that culminates
scenically in a semicircular
wall against the
background of the hill.

The villa's new wing,
which Nicolò Duodo had
built in 1740 from designs
by the Venetian architect
Andrea Tirali.

La Rocca Pisana

Lonigo, Vicenza

At the top of a hill, on the site of a medieval fortress, stands the Pisani villa, which still calls to mind the former castle in its simplicity, the neatness of its structures, and the restrained use of fretwork.

In 1576, the Pisani family – already possessing a "villa for income" at Bagnolo and a "palace for reception" at Lonigo – decided, to reconfirm their authority over the territory of Vicenza, to build another edifice for pure enjoyment, one that would serve as a refuge from the pestilent air of the plague that had broken out that same year in Venice.

"The illustrious segnor Vettor Pisani...," writes Vincenzo Scamozzi, the villa's architect, "despite all the buildings owned by his family in the Bagnoli estates, wanted to build another himself, to have a place near Lonigo for recreation in healthier air. It stands atop a hill called La Rocca, where there are a number of ruins of a fortress. The hill is very lovely to look at, as it is almost perfectly round in form, very pleasant when viewed from other, smaller hills, and detached almost all the way around."

Unlike the Cinquecento farm-villas, in which the needs of both the farmer and prince found their practical reconciliation in the architecture, here the villa dominates the surrounding green plain, as if to express the satisfaction that the Pisani must have felt when gazing out from above onto their vast domain.

It was not until the following century that the agricultural annexes were added to the property. They are hidden from sight, however, located at the entrance of the road that winds around the hill. This circular motif, formerly used by such Quattrocento architects as Francesco di Giorgio Martini, is supposed to allude to the continuity between nature transformed by man, which bears the mark of his rationalizing interventions, and the building itself.

And thus the hill, which provided the building material extracted from a quarry at its base, becomes, together with the villa crowning it, an emblematic example of the fusion between architecture and landscape, fulfilling Scamozzi's ideal of exalting the relationship between house and environment.

Vincenzo Scamozzi's masterpiece, Villa Pisani, sitting "atop a hill known as La Rocca".

The façade of the Rocca
Pisana, with dome
crowning the central room.

Inside, the logic of the architecture, is not disturbed by paintings or decorations, and expresses itself through the modulated flow of light. Traditional villa features are not lacking, however: the staircase in front of the façade, the columned porch, the geometric crowning of the dome, at the top of which is a circular open window. The light that falls from this opening heightens the refined outlines of the niches, hardly interrupted by the mouldings of the doors and windows. The endless wealth of decoration of Palladio's Rotonda is not, therefore, comparable to the severity and geometric rigor of Scamozzi's delightful building, overlooking the plain below almost like a laic sanctuary of the "goddess Healty."

In *The Idea of a Universal Architecture*, Scamozzi wrote: "This building is so harmonious that when one stands in the middle of the main room one has the four cross-views of the four large doors, and those of the loggia and the salons where the light enters the room horizontally and from above, while most of the openings of one wall encounter those of the other…; and as it works with the view, so with the purifying of the air as well."

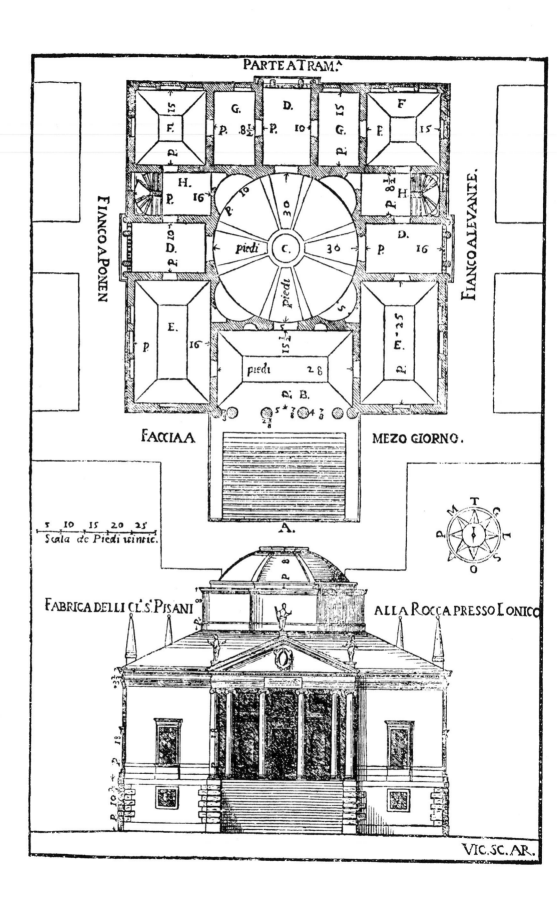

Vincenzo Scamozzi, plan and elevation of the Rocca Pisana (from the Idea of a Universal Architecture, *Venice, 1615, part I, book III).*

Vincenzo Scamozzi
(1552–1616)

Architect, hydraulic engineer, essayist, Vincenzo Scamozzi enjoyed widespread fame, not only in the Venetian Domain but in Central Europe as well. Scamozzi's constant attention to questions of planning and his sensitivity to the lessons taught by Palladio made him one of the most important interpreters of Venetia's "villa culture." In keeping with Palladio's tradition, Scamozzi dedicated a number of pages in his treatise to building materials, in particular to the various kinds of stone that can be used for villas. Sensitive to the value of the environment, Scamozzi at times succeeds in realizing a powerful union between edifice and landscape (such as in the Rocca Pisana), using materials available in the quarries at the site. Vicenza, moreover, was famous for the existence of important quarries in its territories, such as the white stone quarry at Costozza and the yellow stone quarry at Nanto. Palladio too preferred to use, over all other stone except that of Istria, the stone of Vicenza, which is porous, sensitive to light reflections, and rich in pictorial effects, as he well knew from having worked as a stonecutter in his youth.

Villa Molin

Mandria, Padua

At one time, the waters of the Battaglia canal reflected the image of the severe, massive structure of Villa Molin and its majestic, columned pronaos. Now the villa stands smothered by the high embankment, which was raised repeatedly over the centuries. Conceived by Vincenzo Scamozzi according to a square plan, Villa Molin has experienced a fate quite different from that of the Rocca Pisana, which still stands intact and triumphant atop its hill near Lonigo. A pupil of Palladio who followed the teachings of that great architect, Scamozzi also absorbed his mentor's love of landscape, and in his creations he always strove to unite the edifice with the natural environment in a relationship of perfect harmony.

Describing Villa Molin in his book *The Idea of a Universal Architecture*, Scamozzi wrote: "The front of the building looks South-east; in front of it passes the very navigable Bacchiglione river..."

Built in 1597 for the Venetian ambassador Nicolà Molin, the villa was later acquired by some of the most illustrious families of Venice and the mainland: the Pisani, the Sagredos, the Capodilistas, and the Dondi dall'Orologio.

The building's central core consists of the majestic, domed hall that leads on to the four vestibules of the independent apartments on the ground floor. Unfortunately, inside one cannot see and appreciate the harmonious proportions that characteristically make Scamozzi's villas so charming. In fact, unlike the Rocca Pisana, the walls are covered with Seicento frescos which distract one's attention with their exaggerated perspectives and superabundance of decorative elements. The garden must have been very large and impressive, and the fountain, statues, and age-old trees in the park suggest what it might have been like.

Now smothered by the high embankment of the canal, Scamozzi's Villa Molin once dominated the landscape in harmony with the natural environment.

Villa Molin in an eighteenth-century fresco at Villa Emo Capodilista at Selvazzano.

Villa Molin, façade reflecting in the waters of the Bacchiglione.

The central salon with seventeenth-century frescos attributed to Pier Antonio Cerva, which tend illusionistically to amplify the architectural space.

Villa Emo Capodilista
Montecchia di Selvazzano, Padua

The noble Capodilista family possessed vast territories in the Paduan province. In around 1560 they obtained in fee old Montìcula, situated between two small elevations at the edge of the Euganean hills. The particular sort of jursidiction that they exercised over these places found its emblematic expression in the splendid villa erected in 1568 near the old medieval castle.

Dario Varotari, a painter and architect, conceived this highly original edifice, which he decorated himself with a vast cycle of frescos, creating a complex unique in its homogeneity and unity. With the assistance of Aliense and other painters, Varotari brightened the villa's rooms with grotesques, delicate floral decorations, friezes with mythological scenes, and episodes of Roman history. Between great arches one sees the figures of *Sophonisba, Scipio*, and *Antony and Cleopatra*; in other frescos one recognizes all the villas belonging to the Paduan nobility of the time. The allegories in the eighteenth-century landscape rooms represent *Time, Truth*, and *Vice*, while on the ceiling of the ground-floor loggia one finds a new interpretation of the pergola (a common theme in villas that often invokes the richness of wine), with *putti* and animals emerging from the arbor.

The building typology of this edifice is significant, with its square plan and its adherence to a precise symmetry, even in the arrangement of the rooms: four on the ground floor and four on the second floor, with the servants' quarters in the basement. A recurrent inspiration in Cinquecento architecture, the geometry of the square, as Palladio observed, brought out the excellence of a building more than any other form. Vincenzo Scamozzi, in his 1651 work *The Idea of a Universal Architecture*, wrote that "... the square form comes out much more harmonious and commodious... since it takes up much space with great savings in expenses..."

Moreover, the centralized-cubic model, one of the most characteristic types of villa since the Roman era – as Ackerman has pointed out – opens up onto the countryside in a manner analogous to Palladio's Rotonda, thanks to the four views embracing the entire horizon.

Dario Varotari designed and decorated this unusual building that dominates the countryside with its four façades.

On the following pages: The charming staircase leading up to the villa; one of the ground floor loggias decorated with landscapes and grotesques by Dario Varotari and his school.

252

Villa Selvatico
Sant'Elena di Battaglia, Padua

The villa, attributed to Lorenzo Bedogni, is reached by an endless staircase first passes the tenants' houses and then crosses through the park conceived by Giuseppe Jappelli.

Preceded by a majestic staircase, this original construction stands amid picturesque natural surroundings, crowning a small hill. The brilliant arrangement of the park was the work of Giuseppe Jappelli, who practised in the area around 1818.

The villa, built in the late 1500s, in an important foreshadowing of the Baroque style. Showing creative brilliance, the unknown architect abandons the classical compactness of the Renaissance and presents a unique encounter of architectural motifs, giving a glimpse at the strange solutions of the century to follow.

The building is centrally planned, with four façades and a small dome on top; inside it contains an excellent cycle of frescos representing the story of the *Founding of Padua*, commissioned by the marquis Benedetto Selvatico to Luca Ferrari da Reggio. On the ceiling, a painting by Padovanino depicting the *Glory of the House of Selvatico* celebrates the villa's proprietors, who were hosts to illustrious figures, princes, and men of letters.

In the Salon on the first
floor of Villa Selvatico,
Luca da Reggio painted
the fresco representing
the founding of Padua
in 1650.

Luca da Reggio, fresco of
Antenor's Victory over
Valesius.

HIC ODIIS ACTI SVBEVNT BELLA ASPERA BRITI
ANTENOR VALESI SPOLIIS EXVLTAT OPIMIS

259

Villa Garzadori Da Schio

Costozza di Longare, Vicenza

A long staircase, climbing obliquely up the hill and flanked rhythmically by statues and broad terraces, leads majestically up to the Garzadori Da Schio architectural complex. Made up of three nuclei – the so-called Ca' Molina, the manor house and, the small villa known as Grotto of Marinali – it conforms in its structure to the rocky slope of the hill. The artistic quality of the buildings is itself rather modest; what is most striking and fascinating is instead the sheer sense for natural setting in the landscape as well as the interiors. Particularly impressive and original is the little villa at the top, part of which is carved into the rock: inside, one is struck by the harmonious fusion of the natural element and the architectural intervention, so much so that it is difficult to tell where the wall surface ends and the hard rock of the hill begins.

Happily this strange space is lightened by the delicate eighteenth century paintings of Ludovico Dorigny. With deft illusionism, the artist creates crumbling architectures to counterbalance the solidity of the rock and the lively sculptural style of Orazio Marinali, of which the *Neptune* located in the garden is a magnificent example.

From an iconographical point of view the complex seems inspired by the cycle of the seasons and their eternal rotation. Moreover, the Da Schio villa shows a brilliance of perspective and design in the structure of its parks, gardens, and cedargroves. In 1580, Luigi Groto, in a letter to Francesco Trento, wrote: "Never will I forget Costozza, which, had I been in the East..., I would have thought myself in earthly Paradise... Never will I forget those cold wines, which quelled at once the thirst and the heat, and made one wonder whether it was Summer or Winter..." It remains one of the most delightful and most elaborately decorated corners of the Berici hills.

The picturesque complex follows the contour of the hill amid the trees of the park adorned with statues.

*The "Grotto of Marinali"
takes its name from the
sculptor of the statues
adorning it; the frescos
painted on the living
rock are the work of
Ludovico Dorigny.*

*Villa Garzadori, one of the
loggias with Ionic order,
and entrance stairs
adorned with statues.*

Villa Allegri Arvedi
Cuzzano di Grezzana, Verona

Perhaps first built in the 1500s, as a few of the fresco sections attributed to Veronese would seem to indicate, Villa Allegri took on its present aspect over the course of the 1600s.

Stately and grand in appearance, it is particularly striking when observed as a whole – as a single architectural complex. The manor house with its imposing, pretentious façade is in fact of little significance and of modest architectural value. In addition, the villa flanked by annexes and by two interesting towers, had a strict relationship with the surrounding countryside, being essentially a "landowner's house," which oversaw a farming estate that, by the late seventeenth century, included as many as 314 fields.

The villa, which contains frescos by Dorigny inside, is surrounded by an Italian garden and complemented by a picturesque chapel.

The further one goes from Venice, the more one misses the sense of serene harmony that one finds, for example, in the Treviso region, which was particularly attached to the customs of the Serene Republic, and in those territories that had shown themselves willing to embrace the lessons of Andrea Palladio.

In the Verona province, on the other hand, the characteristics of the former feudalism remain. Palladio himself, while working on Santa Sofia a Pedemonte, made his art conform to the idea of the power of the region's patrons.

The manor house, at the center of vast farmlands; the villa is said to be the work of Giovanni Battista Bianchi (1656).

On the following page: The interior of the Salon of Villa Allegri, with frescos by Lodovico Dorigny and perspective wall paintings that were attributed to Francesco Bibiena.

The little Baroque church of San Carlo, with its lively contours, is decorated inside with frescos by Dorigny and paintings by Antonio Balestra.

Villa Rinaldi
Casella d'Asolo, Treviso

On a picturesque slope in the heart of the Asolan hills stands the Villa Rinaldi, a late-Cinquecento building that was later rebuilt, as one may read on the pediment. The villa is mostly famous for its interior decorations which are by Pietro Liberi and Andrea Celesti.

The architecture, on the other hand, is not particularly special, although it manages to create some pleasant scenic effects: balconies, loggias, and decorative details together make up a lively, varied whole which is in harmony with the vast perspectives of the staircases in the gardens. In the façade's tympanum rising above the cornice and surmounted by statues, sits the Rinaldi family coat of arms flanked by two elephants in low relief.

For our history of villas it may be of interest, if not utmost importance, to cite the following reference to the palace and its builders, which we find in an eighteenth-century codex: "The nobleman Francesco Rinaldi..., wanting his descendants to have great memories of him, memories not inferior to those of his forefathers, entrusted his family with the decoration and enlargement of the beautiful palace at Asolo, which is comparable and equal to the splendours of Rome, noteworthy and memorable for its graceful architecture as well as its wealth of marble, its statues carved by the best of sculptors, and its beautiful grotto and fountains, an artistic marvel comparable to those of the Borghese princes of Rome."

The figures on the roof of the Villa Rinaldi correspond to the perspective of the stairs leading to the garden and also follow the rise of the hill.

268

The staircase and rooms of Villa Rinaldi are embellished with statues, stuccowork and frescos by Andrea Celesti and his school (1705–1707).

271

Villa Giovanelli
Noventa Padovana, Padua

The history of this villa has been characterized by a sequence of vicissitudes, an alternation of splendid moments and crises. The Austrian authorities actually once put it up for sale as scrap material.

The long sojourn of Imperial troops had, in fact, damaged it seriously. With the stuccowork partially destroyed, the frescos ruined, and the structures impaired, an eventual renovation must at some point have seemed impossible.

And yet the villa's fame had once been great, as in 1738 when it was host to the King of Poland's daughter, who on an earlier stop had stayed at the Villa Manin in Passariano. It was on this very occasion that, to add to the palace's stateliness and beauty, the Giovanelli brothers, Andrea and Benedetto, embellished the main façade with the solemn pronaos and the statues representing the *Five Senses* dominated by the *Allegory of the Goddess Reason*. The frescos inside underwent changes when the villa came into the hands of Federico Giovanelli, former bishop of Chioggia and Patriarch of Venice, who took measures to remove several paintings deemed too immodest, and replaced them with ones that were religious in inspiration.

Front view of the villa. Attributed to Antonio Gaspari, the patriarch Giovanni Maria Giovanelli had it built in the 1600s.

Detail of the staircase adorned with statues representing the Five Senses and the Goddess Reason; in the foreground, the allegory of Hearing, by Antonio Gai.

272

Villa Foscarini

Stra, Venice

Along the banks of the Brenta there are a great number of buildings that attest to the spread, over the centuries, of the cult of Palladian architecture. One that stands out in particular is the Villa Foscarini at Stra, with its traditional columned portico, which ennobles the customary Venetian residential typology.

Its elegant façade, which is reflected in the river's waters, was a favorite subject of eighteenth-century Venetian engravers (such as Costa and Coronelli). When depicting the villas of Brenta, they liked to emphasize the buildings' relationships with the river, which was always alive with traffic and populated with every imaginable kind of craft.

The series of decorations that grace its interiors are rich and varied. Most of them were executed in 1652, on the occasion of the marriage of Giovanni Battista Foscarini, and the most highly valued are the work of the baroque painter Pietro Ricchi.

In the eighteenth century these were accompanied by other decorative elements and scenic architectures, while the nineteenth century is documented by Romantic themes in Pompeian style. The complex enjoyed its best days in the eighteenth century, when Marco Foscarini was a Procurator and then Doge of Venice. Among his many guests he entertained the Duke of Modena at the villa, as is recorded in the writings of Gaspare Gozzi, another illustrious guest of the Foscarini.

The villa's elegant façade, clearly inspired by Palladio, dominates the Brenta waterway, once alive with every imaginable sort of craft. The villa's interiors contain frescos by Pietro Ricchi and other Seicento painters.

Villa Negri Lattes
Istrana, Treviso

The districts outside the cities, once verdant refuges for urban nobles and patricians, have in our century been often subjected to a chaotic growth in building and development that has transformed the countryside. Green spaces have grown ever smaller, suffocating building complexes that were originally conceived with the idea of receiving large draughts of air from the surrounding country. Today, Villa Lattes, though a victim of these developments, still welcomes us with its lovely annexes and their curvilinear arcades flanking the body of the main residence.

Giorgio Massari seems to have drawn his inspiration in planning the villa (dated 1715) from a sense of refined and rational harmony of rhythm; its beauty is pure and simple, without decorative excess or neoclassical rigidity. The Palladian influence is undeniable, especially in the arcades enclosing the round courtyard, which are strikingly similar to those of Villa Badoer.

Despite the pitiless assault of the modern building trade, Villa Lattes has retained its charm, remaining a unified and harmonious complex with its orchard, fishpond, its lovely garden, its statues, and the family church. Inside, the building – which Massari, significantly, chose as his own residence – contains some curious collections and valuable works of art.

Among other proprietors aside from Massari, we should mention the patron Paolo Tamagnino and the Counts Negri, Massari's heirs and descendants, who in the mid-nineteenth century sold it to the Lattes family.

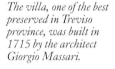

The villa, one of the best preserved in Treviso province, was built in 1715 by the architect Giorgio Massari.

Villa Trissino Marzotto

Trissino, Vicenza

Francesco Muttoni
(1668-1747)

Palladian teachings, especially those concerning villa architecture, were embraced and reinterpreted with originality by the Lombard Francesco Muttoni, born in Porlezza in 1668 and active in Vicenza province. Muttoni also has the distinction of having published, from 1740 to 1747, a reprint of Palladio's work. In Vicenza he built numerous patrician residences such as the Palazzo Repeta, Palazzo Velo, Palazzo Trento now called Valmarana, and other important buildings more public in nature, such as the seat of the Monte di Pietà. He distinguished himself particularly in the construction of villas; in just two years (1714-15) he built Villa Da Porto ("La Favorita") at Monticello di Fara, and in 1724 he built Villa Valmarana Morosini at Altavilla. Muttoni is also responsible for the two porticoed wings that flank the Villa Piovene at Lonedo, as well as for the arrangement of the gardens of the upper villa at Trissino. The architect died in 1747.

The pilasters of the belvedere in the garden in front of the villa, the work of Francesco Muttoni. Girolamo Dal Pozzo; the upper villa and the equestrian courtyard, seen through an arch in the enclosure wall.

The arrival of the Serene Republic of Venice as a political force in the Vicenza province altered local life, sometimes radically, replacing old centers of feudal power and destroying a large number of fortresses and castles.

The house of Trissino, a family of feudal lords of the Agno valley, also adapted to these circumstances, and in the latter half of the fifteenth century, with the extra incentive of the growing charm of city life, they transformed their castle into a peaceful country residence. This constituted the original nucleus of the current, vast Trissino Marzotto complex, which is composed of several building units arranged along the slopes of the hill and was put together in the eighteenth and nineteenth centuries.

Particularly worthy of note is the park, which connects the various structures and surrounds them with enchanting beauty. Francesco Muttoni deserves most of the credit for the marvellous web of walkways that are rich in statues as well as the skilful arrangement of terraces, fish ponds, and hanging gardens, which are distributed at the various levels.

The whole is dominated by a refined, scenic taste, a search for spontaneous dialogue between man and nature, and the aspiration to derive as much enjoyment as possible from a privileged environmental location. The entrance gates by Muttoni and Frigimelica are indeed majestic in appearance, yet characterized here and there by

*Villa Trissino Marzotto.
The pool in front of the
lower villa, with statues
by Marinali.*

odd solutions. Triumphal columns hold up trophies and enclose exquisite wrought iron gates. Unexpected forms in rococo style, elaborate spires, and strange copings all serve to both enliven as well as increase the attractions of this fanciful architectural complex.

Villa Perez Pompei

Illasi, Verona

This imposing structure stands at the center of the large fief of Illasi, which was awarded together with the noble title of Count, by the Doge Priuli on August 12, 1509, to Girolamo I Pompei, a "man at arms" who distinguished himself in the capture and the defense of Mantua. Since the 1400s the Pompei family had possessed properties in the area that were exempt from taxation, and actually the investiture merely made official a long-standing *de facto* situation.

The present-day villa, which replaced an earlier, late-Quattrocento building, was built at the behest of Giugno III Pompei, after a design by "Gio.

Pietro Pozzo, Surveyor, Engineer and Architect of the Court." The central element and right wing were completed in 1737; the left wing, on the other hand, was never built. A construction dating from the sixteenth century, with a Doric loggia on the top floor, was retained instead.

The villa, which is in an excellent state of preservation, is characterized by a grandiose central body marked by two stringcourses and animated by large windows that illuminate the vast, sumptuous interiors.

Almost all of the rooms are decorated with eighteenth-century mythological frescos and furnished with pieces and fabrics of the period.

Also of considerable interest, from an ethno-graphic point of view, are the kitchen, the cellars, the *lissara*, the *giassara*, the stables, and the greenhouses, all of which have been perfectly preserved.

The huge park surrounding the villa dates from the early nineteenth century and is the work of Antonio Pompei. It covers the entire slope of a hill on which stand the ruins of an old medieval castle.

The vastness and richness of the Pompei family's fief – that included many hundreds of tillable fields, vineyards, olive groves, and woods, the revenues from which were regularly supplemented by rents, perpetual leases, and tithes – is reflected in the complex of buildings and the park, the magnificence of which indicates the role that the villa came to assume with time, as the economic and cultural nucleus of the entire region.

It was in this context that the Accademia of Lavina Pompei flourished, counting among its frequenters the likes of Jourdan and Pindemonte.

Aside from the church and the many annexes used for work in the fields, a 1788 list of the "Delightful Gardens and Orchards" in the Pompei domain mentions the "garden with vine pergolas, fruit cellars, greenhouses, thickets, playing fountains, avenues, pools of water, and other delights."

The villa remained in the Pompei family until 1885, when the last member of the line died, and the estate came into the hands of a cousin, Giovanni Perez Pompei.

Villa Loschi Zileri Dal Verme

Biron di Monteviale, Vicenza

In 1734 Nicolò Loschi leveled the hill in order to enlarge the central body of the villa, the lateral parts of which are from an earlier construction.

Not far from Vicenza, in a valley in the Lessini mountains, stretch the grasslands of Biron, which are unparalleled in both their charm and their subtle and continuous variations of green. At the foot of the Monteviale hill, which closes the valley, stands Villa Zileri with its complex of loggias and annexes, the architect of which today remains uncertain.

In 1734 the proprietor, Nicolò Loschi, had the hill leveled and the villa's central part enlarged, incorporating a much older nucleus into the new structures. The architecture does not have a particularly energetic framework, being limited to the rhythm of openings on the outer wall. Divided into three sections, the façade presents an imposing family coat of arms.

One of the more significant and felicitous elements is the dramatic grand staircase that leads up to the *piano nobile* and seems to continue, in parallel fashion, the line of the hill's ascent.

A curiosity to be found on the ground floor is the so-called "Grotto of shells," which, in fact, is connected to a natural grotto in the hill. This grotto, which Alfonso Loschi had built in 1665, strikes one as a most fanciful invention – among other reasons for its strange decoration in shells – that perhaps goes hand in hand with a mentality of jest and surprise.

*Eighteenth-century
drawing concerning the
Salon. The drawing is still
kept at the villa.*

Inside we find the first cycle of frescos that Giambattista Tiepolo realized in the Vicenza province. The frescos express a specific program, moral in tone: we see such themes as *Time discovering Truth, Activity triumphing over Idleness*, the *Virtues*, and so on.

A letter written by Giambattista Tiepolo to Lodovico Faronati on November 17, 1734, tells of the great painter's work. He worked in Villa Loschi Zileri Dal Verme at Biron for three months without stopping.

In these frescos, Tiepolo definitively breaks away from the street-scene style and, drawing on the great Veronese tradition, attains the classicism characteristic of his mature period.

The park was designed by Muttoni but realized by Balzaretti later on, in the then popular romantic, English style, with a balanced distribution of trees, sometimes valuable, and broad meadows.

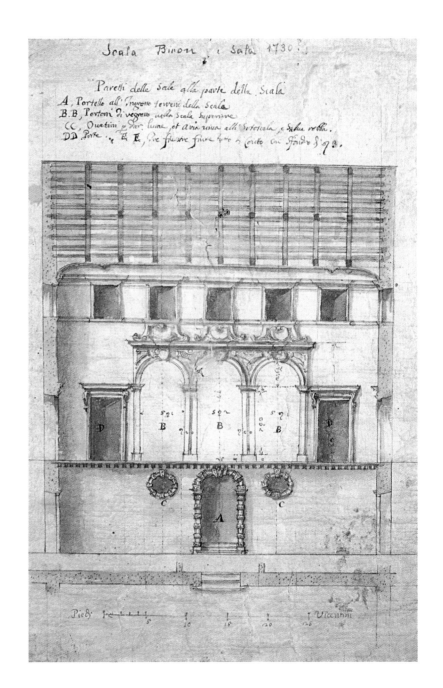

Villa Pisani

Stra, Venice

The majestic Pisani that stands on the banks of the Brenta occupies a special and original position in the ranks of Italian villas. It does not in fact constitute the usual combination of eulogistic concern and economic reality, of lordly ambition and agricultural activity. Grandiose in size and perhaps inspired by Versailles and other European royal palaces, Villa Pisani owes its birth to a specific political event – the accession of Alvise Pisani to the Dogal throne from 1735–41. Through the magnificence of his patrician residence, Doge Pisani wanted to display the wealth, prestige, and high rank of his family.

After the first design – done in the baroque style by Girolamo Frigimelica and preserved in the form of a rare wooden model at the Museo Correr – was abandoned, the definitive realization of the villa was entrusted to Francesco Maria Preti, who tempered the fanciful inventions of his predecessor with a Palladian sense of restraint. Palladian typologies in fact influenced the large central structure of the rear façade, where the customary Ionic pronaos with tympanum stands triumphant, two stories high and echoed in the rest of the façade. The front façade has a central body with a Corinthian order and to the sides, a lower, combined order. Only the arched porticos in the wings, with their rusticated ashlar, can be said symbolically to allude, as Ackerman put it, to the "rusticity of the countryside."

The villa is most famous for its park, in which one finds a wealth of architectural caprices such as fountains, gates, portals, and an endless store of inventions, like the celebrated botanical labyrinth. More out of keeping with the whole complex is the rectangular water basin that extends from the back of the villa towards the stables; it was, in fact, built right after the Second World War, for experiments in hydraulics.

The villa's interiors are richly decorated with frescos and paintings by Jacopo Amigoni, Fabio Canal, Giambattista Crosato, Jacopo Guarana, Francesco Simonini, Sebastiano Ricci, Giuseppe Zais, and Francesco Zuccarelli, while in the central salon Giambattista Tiepolo in 1767 painted a fantastic vision known as the *Glory of the house of Pisani*. In my opinion the main protagonist of this composition is the little boy held in his mother's arms in the lower section; this boy is Almorò Pisani, son of Alvise, and he would become a passionate art lover.

This stately and highly symbolical palace received among its guests the Counts of the North, King Gustave of Sweden, Napoleon, Viceroy Eugenio of Italy, Maria Luisa of Parma, Maximillian of the Habsburgs, and many other illustrious figures.

This monumental complex truly deserves the title of "Villa of the Doges," in that it was erected to celebrate Alvise Pisani's accession to the Dogal throne in 1735.

"Few are the foreigners, even those from far away, who do not know the Brenta to be a delightful river, running from the lagoons to the city of Padua, along whose banks stand so many palaces, gardens, and pleasant retreats, that one could never ask for anything more magnificent or delectable. Everyone rushes there, at different times, to the amusement of the countryside" (Carlo Goldoni, Il Prodigo. Momolo sulla Brenta, Preface, 1739).

*The park of Villa Pisani,
and a garden structure.*

294

Three photographs of one of the garden structures with a lookout, in the park of Villa Pisani.

The colonnade that crosses
the ground floor of Villa
Pisani.

One of the two courtyards
with simulated statues
painted in fresco by Fabio
Canal and portraying the
Twelve Caesars.

*Villa Pisani, the
Ballroom, frescoed from
1760–62 by Giambattista
Tiepolo, Pietro Visconti,
and Jacopo Guarana.*

*Giambattista Tiepolo,
Fresco on the Ballroom
ceiling, representing
the Apotheosis of the
Pisani family.*

*Villa Pisani, the Room
of Bacchus, frescos by
Jacopo Guarana and
quadraturist collaborators;
on the ceiling the
Marriage of Bacchus
and Ariadne.*

Villa Manin
Passariano, Udine

The founding of Palmanova and the resulting climate of security that came to this border territory in the seventeenth century, favored an increase in land development as well as the building of canals and roads. The economic rebirth of the Friuli plain also encouraged the Manin family to build their residence in Passariano, and it retains something of the air of a medieval castle, with its tower and drawbridge.

Having received a title of nobility in 1651, Ludovico Manin worked out a project aimed at making the villa an emblem of the prestige his family had attained, as well as a vital nucleus of the vast territories acquired. For the realization of this design he apparently turned to Baldassare Longhena, an architect famous for reorganizing the lands on which he executed his projects. The edifice ultimately took more than a century to build, with modifications and reconstructions that compromised its unity and stylistic harmony. It was above all during the 1700s that the villa was restructured and decorated in a rococo vein to make it conform to the new tastes of the period.

Thus, from a utilitarian villa it was transformed into a place of amusement and reception, a monument to the power of the Mann family as well as to the Republic of Venice, being the first stop for voyagers arriving from across the Alps on their way to the capital of the Republic.

The eighteenth-century intervention is attributed to the architect Giovanni Ziborghi, who also saw to the decoration, the layout of the gardens and fountains, and gave more solid and elegant forms to the loggias, porticos, and granaries. The changes brought to the villa's physiognomy and the refinement of its structures did not, however, alter its essential function as an agricultural and commercial center. Aided by the local roads and by numerous navigable canals, the Manin residence had in front of it a large, round courtyard used for receiving and sorting out the produce of the region, which was then sent onto Venice, or to its colonies, across the sea.

To better serve their commercial function, the annexes were equipped both to lodge and entertain

Built by a family of merchants that acquired nobility through its wealth, this villa served as a stopping point for monarchs from transalpine nations on their way to Venice. In this photograph, the villa is seen from across the canal separating it from the road and from the round piazza in front of it.

with performances the crowd that periodically converged in the inner square of Villa Manin. Like triumphal arches, the majestic portals leading to the courtyard were always open, allowing passage to and from the public road and giving the villa a sense of collectivity.

Adorned with fish pools and statues, and flanked by the comfortable guest-lodgings, the courtyard is surrounded by the curved wings of the annexes, which give a sense of unity to the entire complex.

In order to emphasize the public-oriented purpose of the villa, the Manins decided that their family chapel should be "for common use." For particular religious holidays the peasants and proprietors participated together in the services, even though the nobles preferred to take their seats in the sacristy connected to the chapel by iron gates.

In order to be able to suggest the most up-to-date ideas to his patrons, the architect Giovanni Ziborhi traveled continuously throughout Italy and abroad. At Passariano he recreated the same atmosphere as in Paris or Vienna. We are, moreover, in a region fairly international in flavor, as attested by its frequent relations with the transalpine feudal nobility and the Friulian custom of using German coins alongside Venetian ones.

Once decorated with a treasure of artworks, today in the rooms and halls of the palatial Manin villa we can still see elegant rococo stuccowork and the strange polychrome decorations of illusory curtains,

Villa Manin. A play of marble and stuccowork in transalpine style depicting a mock door on the piano nobile *of the building.*

The grand staircase adorned with statues.

which seem to reflect a sensibility closer to Austrian rococo than to the Italian style. Still in a state of perfect preservation are the frescos of Ludovico Dorigny on the ceilings of the ground floor.

Even though some of the wealth and magnificence of the Manin residence has since been lost – like the park constructions, the paintings, tapestries, and furniture – the villa still stands today as a testimony of the typically eighteenth-century ambitions and aspirations to both theatricality and merriment that made this complex one of the most famous and admired in all of Venetia.

Villa Manin; the Montagnola. A path in the park with statues.

313

Villa Cordellina
Montecchio Maggiore, Vicenza

In around the mid-1700s, Carlo Cordellina, a Venetian lawyer who handled official assignments for the Republic, decided to have a villa built in the environs of Vicenza, in a place where he would have both the Lessini and Berici mountains in the background. But the spot that Cordellina picked out did not fulfil the essential requirements for the ideal realization of the project, since on that site the villa would have had no available water.

So great was his desire to achieve that ancient ideal of a villa, already realized by Palladio at Maser, that Cordellina, envisioning gardens, orchards, and fountains as complements to the architecture, tapped the waters of a spring found right there in the side of the hill. Thus he was able to benefit not only his own lands, but the entire town of Montecchio, creating a tank into which water flowed for public use.

Cordellina attached his name to the architecture realized by Giorgio Massari between 1735 and 1760, which proved to be one of the most eminent examples of the Palladian revival that characterized much of the villa construction of that century.

The culture of the noble Venetian who chose to realize his humanistic dream in the villa (almost as though it were his own creation) has its counterpart in both the architecture and the decorations. Since he also wanted this to be a meeting-place for the most enlightened gentlemen of the city and the nearby villas, the generous patron had guest-quarters built that were almost on a par in elegance with the master's house.

The Montecchio complex was closely bound up with the benefits offered by the surrounding countryside, and expresses a solid relationship with farming activity; the very statues themselves speak of agriculture, as well as the reliefs of deities, the allegories of the seasons, and the abundance of fruit offered in the vases atop the pilasters of the gates.

The same spirit that inspired the first authors of the villas in the Venetia, is here manifest in the frescos of the Salon, which were commissioned in 1743 from Giambattista Tiepolo. These constitute the second cycle of the series he painted in the Vicenza province. On the ceiling of this "temple"

The work of Giorgio Massari, an eighteenth-century interpreter of Palladian principles, this villa, decorated with frescos by Giambattista Tiepolo and sculptures by the studio of the Bonazza, was an ideal meeting place for highly-educated aristocrats and scholars.

Giambattista Tiepolo. The Triumph of Virtues, Nobility and Intelligence over Error (1743–1744), fresco on the ceiling of the Salon of Villa Cordellina.

dedicated to human intelligence, we find a representation of *The light of intelligence putting to flight the shadows of ignorance* (an obvious homage to the century of the Enlightenment), while on the walls we find a eulogy of the virtue and ethics of villa life in the representation of the *Mercy of Alexander and Scipio*. A theme also present in such other Palladian constructions as the one at Fanzolo.

The perfect harmony of this complex is further confirmed by the architect's desire, in determining the correct organization of space, to take acoustical values into account, so that it would be possible and ideal to hold concerts in any of the rooms. In 1801, in his *Memories of the life of Carlo Cordellina*, Giambattista Fontanella wrote of the villa: "I shall always remember Villa Cordellina at Montecchio, where generous hospitality was the custom…, where liberality, life's comforts, the elimination of all labels and fastidious ceremony, and a joyful, noble spirit of merriment made it the delight of all guests."

With the fall of Venice and the resulting spiritual impoverishment and loss of ancient ideals, this need to live "in harmony" also eventually died out, to the point that around the mid-nineteenth century a law was passed that levied specific taxes on luxury buildings, thus encouraging the abandonment or even demolition of many villas that were not sufficiently profitable.

Villa Cordellina, the scene of so much culture, harmony, elegance, and aristocratic ideals, was initially abandoned and then revived for industrial and productive ends. The grand salon became crowded with structures necessary for the cultivation of silkworms, damaging the architecture, the stuccowork, and the frescos. Finally, in 1954 the philanthropist Vittorio Lombardi provided for its restoration. Today the villa, under the care of the regional government, is used for cultural events.

Giambattista Tiepolo. The Mercy of Alexander, fresco on a wall of the Salon of Villa Cordellina.

Villa Marcello
Levada di Piombino Dese, Padua

Surrounded by nearly twelve and a half acres (five hectares) of park, Villa Marcello at Levada, with its refined furnishings and gardens, constitutes one of the best preserved examples of the eighteenth-century Venetian villa, symbol of the rebirth of Palladian art. Famous for having hosted illustrious members of royal families over the course of its history, today it still belongs to the descendants of the Venetian noble house of Marcello.

Crowned by an elegant tympanum, the central body of the edifice is developed on two levels: the upper one is cadenced by an order of Ionic half-columns, while the lower one is connected with the porticoed wings that enclose the Italian garden.

Stately and majestic, the central salon extends over two stories, and has frescos of powerful scenes from ancient history, painted between 1750 and 1755 by Giambattista Crosato.

Monumental eighteenth-century complex with Italian garden in front and flanked by two porticoed wings.

*Villa Marcello. Salon
with frescos by
Giambattista Crosato
depicting Campapses in
Apelle's studio and the
Mercy of Alexander.*

*Opposite:
Giambattista Crosato,
fresco of the Wedding
of Alexander.*

322

Giambattista Crosato
(1686–1758)

The painter and decorator had his earliest experience in art in Venice and Turin. An esteemed scene-painter, Crosato also distinguished himself as a fresco-painter for villas: Villa Algarotti at Mestre, Villa Albrizzi at Preganziol, and Villa Marcello at Piombino Dese.

Villa Pisani
called "La Barbariga"
Stra, Venice

Near the left bank of the Brenta river, straight and solid, stands the villa that once belonged to Chiara Pisani, who became the wife of Filippo Barbarigo, hence the name "la Barbariga." The noble lady wanted her memory to be associated with the beautifully refined garden that she herself designed in the English style, and in the middle of which stands a clock tower.

The broad loggias, the side wings, and the stables were all completed at around the end of the eighteenth century.

Inside the main body the rather small rooms are decorated in exquisitely multicolored stuccowork; the tiles of the fireplaces, the ceramics, the mirrors, the frescos, and the chinoiseries all help to preserve the villa's characteristic atmosphere of eighteenth-century Venetian aristocracy.

Hare coursing was once famous here and was organized by various different noble Venetian families. The hunt has always been one of the appeals that villa life, the country, the woods, and the hills had for nobles, who usually lived in the city and in holiday seasons could rediscover the pleasure of using weapons, something directly connected to their aristocratic origins.

The hunt was an occasion for festive meetings and gatherings that often ended in great banquets and dances on the lawn. Villa Barbariga is still an eloquent document of this custom, with its whole series of sculptures of hunters and loyal dog, which populate the loggias and the garden's walkways.

This villa, with its low, elongated structure, follows the course of the Brenta river. Particularly elegant are the two eighteenth-century wings flanking the seventeenth-century central construction.

On the following pages: Interior of a loggia enlivened by statues of hunters, and a room decorated in delicate stuccowork in the finest Venetian tradition.

Villa Valmarana ai Nani

Vicenza

This villa (1655–70) owes its name to the statues adorning the enclosure wall, which are attributed to Giambattista Bendazzoli; in the 1700s the surrounding structures were added. The complex is most famous for the frescos by Tiepolo.

In the mid-seventeenth century the Venetian jurist Giovanni Maria Bertolo chose the crest of this charming hill as the place to begin a series of constructions that had no direct connection with farming activity. The complex was built exclusively for the purpose of providing leisurely pleasures and fulfilling the cultural ambitions of the nobleman who, in bestowing his collection of books to the city of Vicenza, founded the library that still bears his name today.

The villa, known as "Valmarana ai Nani," was not finished until one century after it was started. At that time Venetian architects, among whose names we find those of Massari and Muttoni, built the guest quarters and the stables, thus completing the complex with as much unity as possible.

The famous caricatural statues of dwarfs that crown the enclosure wall appear to have been executed by the sculptor Giambattista Bendazzoli, probably from drawings by Giambattista Tiepolo. The *palazzina* and guest-quarters of the Valmarana complex contain frescos painted by Giambattista and Giandomenico Tiepolo, father and son, around the middle of the century.

Wolfgang Goethe, in his *Voyage to Italy* (1816–17), wrote the following about Villa Valmarana: "Today

Giambattista Tiepolo. Fresco of Rinaldo abandoning Armida, in the Room of the Jerusalem Delivered at Villa Valmarana.

Detail of the scene of Eurybates and Talthybios leading Briseis to Agammennon, in the Room of the Iliad.

I saw Villa Valmarana, which Tiepolo decorated, giving full rein to his talents and shortcomings: he is not as successful in the sublime style as in the natural, but in the latter there are some splendid things. As a wall-painter in general he is full of ingeniousness and resources."

In these works the two different artistic personalities display their distinguishing characteristics. The works by Giambattista, who is still immersed in ancient myths and Renaissance literary themes, are the episodes taken from Ariosto's *Orlando Furioso* and Tasso's *Jerusalem Delivered*, and, in a more spectacular vein, the visions from the *Aeneid* and the *Iliad* in the rooms of the *palazzina*.

The art of Giandomenico, on the other hand, belongs to the bourgeois world. In the frescos in the guest-quarters he shows himself to be an acute observer of everyday life in the country: we see peasants at meal-time and at rest, an old woman selling eggs at the edge of the road, and peasant-women going to the city. But these scenes are placed beside others with dances, gypsies and mountebanks, chinoiseries, and exotic characters amid picturesque landscapes, rococo decorations, and neo-Gothic frames that bear witness to the complexity and crisis of the times.

Guest quarters of Villa Valmarana, the Room of the Gothic Pavilion, with frescos by Giambattista Tiepolo and Gerolamo Mengozzi Colonna.

Left: Fresco of the Declaration of Love, in the room of the Gothic Pavilion. Right: fruit offerings to a lunar deity, in the Chinese Room.

The Painters Tiepolo

Giambattista Tiepolo and his son, Giandomenico, played a prominent role in the fresco decorations of Venetian Villas in the eighteenth century. Born in Venice in 1696, Giambattista Tiepolo was one of the most celebrated artists of his time. His first works date from around 1716. In the 1730s he was active in Milan (Palazzo Archinti) and Bergamo (Colleoni Chapel), after which he painted the Stories of Cleopatra in fresco in the Palazzo Labia in Venice. After devoting himself, from 1740 to 1750, to easel painting, he resumed painting fresco cycles on a grand scale: after 1751 he was in Würzburg at the imperial palace, and in 1754–55 he decorated the ceiling of the Venetian church of the Pietà. From this same period date his paintings in the villas; in 1757, together with his son he frescoed the rooms of Villa Valmarana near Vicenza, around 1761 he painted the Glories of the House of Pisani in the villa at Stra, and in 1743 he was at Villa Cordellina in Montecchio Maggiore. Having gone to Spain at the request of Charles III, he died in Madrid in 1770. Giandomenico (Venice 1727–1804) often collaborated with his father, and followed him to Spain on his unfortunate voyage. The most memorable of his works are the frescos in the guest-quarters of Villa Valmarana and his own country house at Zianigo (1791–94).

Giandomenico Tiepolo. Fresco of the peasant's family at meal time, in the Room of Rustic Scenes in the Guest house of Villa Valmarana.

On the following page: Peasant at rest and woman spinning.

*Giandomenico Tiepolo,
fresco of the Charlatan, in
the Room of Carnival
Scenes in the guest house of
Villa Valmarana.*

*Giandomenico Tiepolo,
detail of landscape, in the
Room of the Iliad.*

*Illusionistic painting by
Gerolamo Mengozzi
Colonna in the Room of
Carnival Scenes; the
figure of the Negro with a
tray has been attributed to
Giambattista Tiepolo.*

Villa Pompei Carlotti

Illasi, Verona

A stately building in the heart of the region, Villa Carlotti assumed its present appearance in 1737, following the reconstruction by Alberto and Alessandro Pompei, designed by the latter. Often in this history of Villa architecture, we have seen how important a role the proprietor, with his personal tastes and individual ideas, played by intervening directly in the planning, or influencing the architect with suggestions and advice.

This tradition was amply documented in Palladio's *Four Books of Architecture*, which had among its protagonists some of the most illustrious political figures active in cultural matters, such as Giangiorgio Trissino and Alvise Cornaro. There are probably countless other villas, thought now to be anonymously designed, that were probably built based on the design of the patrician proprietor, with the help of local workmen.

View of the Villa Pompei Carlotti, based on a design by the amateur architect and proprietor Alessandro Pompei.

Alessandro Pompei was himself an amateur in architecture, the chosen art of the nobility, and a faithful interpreter of the classical Cinquecento tradition. Particularly attuned to the Palladian tradition, he drew his inspiration, in designing his own residence, from the work of the great architect, as we can see in the pronaos with its Doric columns and the balustrade adorned with mytho-logical sculptures. The villa was then decorated by Antonio Balestra, one of the most famous painters in the Verona province at the time.

Yet, alongside the revival of the classical style, in this villa we also find evidence of the continuance of ancient feudal military tradition, clearly manifest in the two turrets flanking the main façade and emphasizing its image of power.

Villa Gera

Conegliano, Treviso

Giuseppe Jappelli
(1783–1832)

An architect and engineer, Giuseppe Jappelli worked mostly in Padua and the surrounding territory. He collaborated with Selva and in 1836 went to England. A rather eclectic spirit, he realized buildings in the neoclassical style, such as Villa Gera in Conegliano and the Caffè Pedrocchi (1816–1831) in Padua, as well as other significant projects in the neo-gothic style, such as the Pedrocchino. Particularly sensitive to the powers of the landscape, he planned the layout of numerous parks and gardens, such as at Villa Papfava in Bastia, Villa Cittadella in Saonara, or at Villa Wollemburg in Loreggia. He died in 1832.

Around 1830 the wealthy Gera family, perhaps under the influence of the fervid political climate present at the time, decided to build, on the hill of Conegliano, a villa proportionate to its own ambitions. For the task they turned to some of the more celebrated artists of the time: the pictorial decoration was entrusted to Giovanni Demin, while Giuseppe Jappelli designed the main house, a majestic neoclassical edifice more academic than Palladian in its inspiration.

Standing next to the medieval towers of an old castle, the villa dominates the landscape with its grandiose pronaos, which is reminiscent of the façade of an ancient temple and uncommonly imposing for a building of Venetia.

It seems strange that Jappelli, usually so sensitive to environmental features, here ignored all relation between the architecture and the landscape, presenting a result that is rather inconsistent and contradictory. Taking advantage of the slope of the hill, he could have emphasized the site's "picturesque" qualities, creating fantastic grottos, fountains, and statues (as he had done in the Padua province), and inserting a neo-Gothic building that would have been more attuned to the nearby ruins.

Apparently, in realizing the Gera villa the architect had to set aside his own ideals and give way to the pressing requests of his patrons. They wanted to manifest their social and economic predominance with this monumental villa-temple.

This monumental neoclassical villa atop the hill of Conegliano was built in 1830 by Giuseppe Jappelli in glorification of the Gera family.
The villa's proximity to the Castle of Conegliano seems to suggest the long process during which villa architecture slowly replaces the castles that once dominated the landscape of Venetia.

Villa Gera. Interior of the loggia that looks out onto the landscape of Conegliano.

Giovanni Demin, the Helvetians being subjugated by Caesar (1837), fresco in the villa's Salon.

349

Villa Revedin
Castelfranco Veneto, Treviso

The park with greenhouses. The villa's ballroom, painted by Giacomo Casa (1864–65). Subsequent pages: the grand staircase, and one of the two horses in the green amphitheater.

From the 1400s up until 1600, the place called "Paradiso," at the edge of Castelfranco, contained a residence belonging to the Corner family. In 1607, this was replaced by a villa more adapted to the new economic demands and to the prestige of its proprietors.

Thus Vincenzo Scamozzi built, for Nicolò Cornaro, a huge building complex consisting of two symmetrical edifices, an annex, and a garden filled with valuable statues. Yet this architectural work also was short-lived; it was demolished around the

mid-nineteenth century, and in the area of Scamozzi's annexes the grandiose Revedin palace was erected from designs by Giambattista Meduna (1855). The complex includes stable, fish ponds, and a picturesque lake. Facing the beautiful, immense park – designed by Antonio Caregaro Negrin – is the main façade of the new villa.

In the middle of the park is an impressive green amphitheater rhythmically, which is adorned by an unbroken sequence of statues by Marinali, and by two monumental horses marking the entrance.

Index of Names, Places and Subjects

Index of Villas

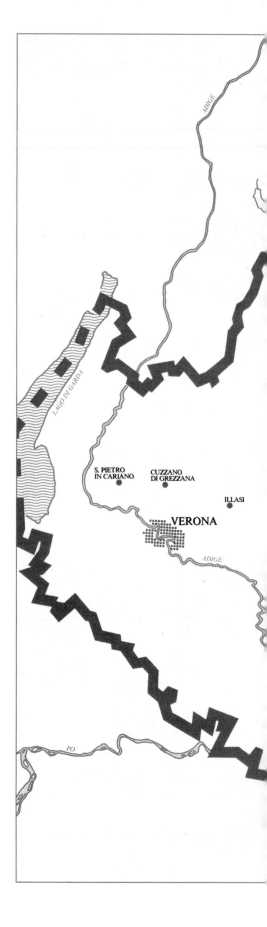

BRENTA

PIAVE

TAGLIAMENTO

UDINE

PORDENONE

PASSARIANO

CONEGLIANO

PALMANOVA

BRENTA

PIAVE

PORTOGRUARO

LONEDO

ENE

ASOLO   MASER   CUSIGNANA

BASSANO

MONTEBELLUNA

ALTIVOLE

FANZOLO

CASTELFRANCO
VENETO   ISTRANA

LIVENZA

TREVISO

TESINA

CARMIGNANO

CITTADELLA

RONCADE

SAN DONÀ
DI PIAVE

QUINTO
VICENTINO

PIOMBINO DESE

LUGHIGNANO

PREGANZIOL

SILE

LE

VICENZA

PIAZZOLA
SUL BRENTA

ZIANIGO

LONGARE

MALCONTENTA

MURANO

MONTEGALDELLA

NOVENTA
PADOVANA

MIRA

VENEZIA

MONTECCHIA
DI SELVAZZANO

STRA

ALBETTONE

ROVOLON

PADOVA

MANDRIA

IGLIA

LUVIGLIANO

BRENTA

AGUGLIARO

NOVENTA
VICENTINA

BATTAGLIA
TERME

IORE

ARQUÀ PETRARCA

NANA

ESTE

MONSELICE

PONTECASALE

BACCHIGLIONE

BAGNOLI DI SOPRA

CAVÁRZERE

ADIGE

ROVIGO

ANDA

PO

FRATTA POLESINE